Signature Dishes of
AMERICA

—— RECIPES AND CULINARY TREASURES ——
FROM HISTORIC HOTELS AND RESTAURANTS

SHERRY MONAHAN

Globe
Pequot

ESSEX, CONNECTICUT

Globe Pequot

An imprint of Globe Pequot, the trade division of
The Rowman & Littlefield Publishing Group, Inc.
4501 Forbes Blvd., Ste. 200
Lanham, MD 20706
www.rowman.com

Distributed by NATIONAL BOOK NETWORK

British Library Cataloguing in Publication Information available

Library of Congress Cataloging-in-Publication Data
Names: Monahan, Sherry, author.
Title: Signature dishes of America : recipes and culinary treasures from historic hotels and
    restaurants / Sherry Monahan.
Description: Essex, Connecticut : Globe Pequot, [2023] | Includes index.
Identifiers: LCCN 2023006840 (print) | LCCN 2023006841 (ebook) | ISBN 9781493072644 (cloth)
    | ISBN 9781493072651 (electronic)
Subjects: LCSH: Cooking, American. | Restaurants—United States—History. | Hotels—United
    States—History. | LCGFT: Cookbooks.
Classification: LCC TX715 .M8113 2023 (print) | LCC TX715 (ebook) | DDC 641.597—dc23/
    eng/20230310
LC record available at https://lccn.loc.gov/2023006840
LC ebook record available at https://lccn.loc.gov/2023006841

∞™ The paper used in this publication meets the minimum requirements of American National Standard for Information Sciences—Permanence of Paper for Printed Library Materials, ANSI/NISO Z39.48-1992.

Contents

PREFACE

Taste and smell are two senses that can evoke powerful memories, and many of them are good. We've all had bad experiences, too, but let's not go down that rabbit hole, and focus on the good ones. Do you remember visiting a place and eating out and can still almost smell it or taste it? That's how powerful food can be and this book sets out to help you re-create some of those yummy memories, or even make some new ones.

I've loved cooking and dining out for decades, and sometimes I'm bold enough to ask a chef for a recipe because I liked the dish so much. My family and friends just roll their eyes when I do, but they indulge me. I decided to write this book and amass a collection of recipes from across America that I hope you'll enjoy creating.

I've tried to include as many of these historic dishes as I could find, but sometimes even the best researchers can't find them all. Maybe my readers will share some that I've missed and can be added to future editions or will make up a whole new book!

Being a culinary historian and professional genealogist led to some fun and history for some of America's most popular foods.

INTRODUCTION

There are so many iconic, classic, and well-known dishes that chefs and cooks created that have lasted well over a century. Many of the dishes we know and love have come from some of the most historic restaurants and hotels across America. Some of them still remain, while others have only their signature dish as proof of their existence. Some dishes may not be new creations, but a hotel or restaurant brought it to the forefront and made it their signature dish. Popularity played a big role when some chefs were creating their dishes. Some made a humble home dish a popular item that became an American icon. Hotels and restaurants across America have signature dishes and culinary traditions that have been a part of their history.

Sometimes new creations had their roots in a similar dish from the past, but due to lack of ingredients, newly available ingredients, or preparation style, they led to a completely new recipe with shades of its past. Over the decades several of these recipes were featured in newspapers or travel books published by the Ford Motor Company or written by Duncan Hines. Yes, Mr. Hines, as in the baking company, was a food lover who traveled a lot and published a large collection of treasured recipes from hotels and restaurants.

This is meant to be a fun foray into historic foods across the country, not a complete in-depth study, so dig in and enjoy some tasty tidbits behind some of America's historic and signature dishes.

BREAKFASTS *and* BREADS

EGGS BENEDICT

1837, DELMONICO'S, NEW YORK, NEW YORK

Many know this famed New York City steakhouse, but most probably don't realize the number of culinary delights that originated here. This is just one of them, but you'll find more in other sections.

The original Delmonico's was opened in New York City in 1837 by brothers John and Peter Delmonico at Beaver and South William Streets and was known as the Citadel. While they later opened other locations in the city, the Citadel is the only remaining restaurant. The Delmonico family and their staff set many of the restaurant standards that are used today and were reportedly the first to use menus and tablecloths and serve women in private dining rooms. And, of course, the food and its excellence were known far and wide. In fact, places all across the country, despite having no association with Delmonico's, named their restaurants Delmonico's and rode on the coattails of the original New York one.

Several men served as the restaurant's chefs and maîtres d'hotel through the years, including Alessandro/Alexander Filippini, Eugene Laperruque, F. A. Archambault, Charles Ranhofer, and Prosper Grevillot, who worked under Ranhofer for twenty years. While all of these men contributed to the history and food of Delmonico's, Charles Ranhofer had the most influence. Cooking was in his DNA and he grew up in France—his father owned the Café et Restaurant du Commerce, and his grandfather was also a chef.

Born in St. Denis, France, in 1836, Charles was sent to Paris at the age of twelve by his father to learn under some of the best experts. He learned pastry making in the kitchen of Monsieur Fleuret, of the Boulevard de la Madeleine, for three years. He then worked for the Prince d'Hénin and Count of Alsace and then moved back to Paris. He arrived in America in 1856 and worked for the Russian Consul, traveled to New Orleans, and then went back to Paris in 1860. Delmonico's first hired him in 1862 to work at their new 14th Street and Fifth Avenue location. He left America in 1876 to start his own restaurant in France, but returned in 1879 and was hired back by Lorenzo Delmonico and remained with the restaurant for nearly thirty-four years. He is credited with creating many of Delmonico's well-known culinary delights between 1862 and 1899.

Ranhofer was the first French chef to bring the grandeur of his country's cuisine to America. He is also the author of a detailed cookbook called *The Epicurean*, published in 1894, based on his time cooking at Delmonico's. Ranhofer was quoted as saying, "Man must eat. It is a necessity. Then why not make it a pleasure instead of a pain by the consumption of what is unpalatable and a menace to health through indigestion?" Another of Delmonico's chefs, Alessandro Filippini, also authored two cookbooks, one of which was titled *The Delmonico Cook Book*, after he left their employ in the 1890s.

According to Delmonico's, Eggs Benedict was created in the 1860s when Mrs. LeGrand Benedict, a regular patron of the restaurant, found nothing to her liking on the menu. She wanted something new to eat for lunch so she discussed her options with chef Charles Ranhofer, who then created the dish.

Then there's the Waldorf Hotel's version, which claims that their head waiter, Oscar Tschirky, created it. According to that version of the recipe's creation, the result was a collaboration between Lemuel Benedict, a Wall Street broker and regular Waldorf patron, and Tschirky in 1894. The story claims that after a night celebrating with friends, Benedict ordered "some buttered toast, crisp bacon, two poached eggs, and a pitcher of Hollandaise sauce." According to the Waldorf-Astoria, Tschirky was impressed and wanted to put an even better version on the Waldorf menu. He named it Eggs Benedict and substituted ham and a toasted English muffin.

However, that would put the creation a year after it appeared in Ranhofer's book, which was copyrighted in 1893 and published a year later. On top of that, Charles Delmonico sent a letter to Ranhofer after reviewing the manuscript in February 1893 (a copy of that letter is in his book). If that's the case, then Tschirky could not have created Eggs Benedict at the Waldorf. It's also interesting to note that a recipe for Eggs Benedict does not appear in Tschirky's cookbook, which was published in 1896.

A third version claimed that a Commodore Benedict went to Delmonico's and wanted a hangover cure and that Eggs Benedict was created for him.

Now, the truth usually lies somewhere in between different versions of a story. I think Julia Child stumbled upon that. She discussed the creation in her 1999 cookbook, *Julia's Breakfasts, Lunches, and Suppers*. She wrote that she originally thought the recipe was created by the New York Yacht Club's (N.Y.Y.C.) Commodore E. C. Benedict, but wanted to verify that. After checking, she wrote, "However, a recent check with the club's librarian, Sohei Hohri, and with Mrs. Allan Butler of Vineyard Haven, Massachusetts, has set the record straight. It seems it wasn't Mr. Benedict (who wasn't the commodore at the N.Y.Y.C., but somewhere else), but his cousin, Mrs. LeGrand Benedict. Mrs. Butler's great-aunt invented the dish, and the place wasn't the N.Y.Y.C. but Delmonico's, an elegant place to lunch at the turn of the century. Mrs. Benedict, bored with the luncheon menu, asked the maître d'hôtel to suggest something new; he asked her if she had any ideas . . . and, just like that, she said, 'What if you put a slice of ham on half an English muffin, and a poached egg on the ham, and hollandaise sauce on the egg, and truffles on top?' And lo, a star was born."

Now, it is possible that that maître d'hôtel she mentioned was Oscar Tschirky before he left for the Waldorf. So, that's the complex story of Eggs Benedict. What we do know is that it appears as if it was created at Delmonico's, and so this is the recipe from Ranhofer's cookbook.

SERVES 2

1 English muffin

2 eggs

Salt and pepper to taste

2 pieces (⅛-inch-thick) cooked ham, round shaped

½ cup Hollandaise sauce

1. Begin by making the Hollandaise sauce.

2. Prepare the English muffin by cutting it in half crosswise and then toast, but do not brown. Place in a 325°F oven to keep warm while you poach the eggs.

3. To poach the eggs, fill a medium-size saucepot with cold water and bring to a gentle boil. Season boiling water with 1 tablespoon of salt and then add 1 tablespoon of white wine vinegar. Stir the water with a whisk until swirling.

4. Crack the eggs into individual small bowls. Lower each bowl and gently drop the eggs into the water. Turn the heat down to a gentle simmer.

5. Cook the eggs for 2 minutes, then check them. If they are firm to the touch, remove from the water with a slotted spoon; if they wobble, return to the water for another 10 seconds.

6. Remove the eggs to a paper towel–lined plate to drain excess moisture. Turn the eggs presentation side up, and season with salt and pepper.

7. Place the eggs over the ham and muffins, and cover with Hollandaise sauce.

HOLLANDAISE SAUCE
MAKES ABOUT 1 CUP

3 egg yolks

2 teaspoons white wine vinegar

1 cup unsalted butter, melted

1 tablespoon lemon juice

Sea salt and freshly ground black pepper to taste

1. Place water in a large saucepan and bring it to a boil, then reduce to a simmer. Either use a double boiler or put a large stainless or heatproof bowl over the saucepan, but do not let the water touch it.

2. Add the egg yolks to the bowl and then the vinegar. Whisk until it becomes foamy, but not too hot. If it does get too hot, take it off the water and beat to cool it down.

3. When you have a gold, airy foam, remove the pan from the heat.

4. Slowly whisk in the melted butter until it's all combined and it looks like mayonnaise.

5. Whisk in the lemon juice and add salt and pepper to taste. You can thin it down with warm water from the pan if the sauce gets too thick.

6. Cover and set aside.

DON'S BIG MESS

1936, WHITE'S RESTAURANT, SALEM, OREGON

According to White's Restaurant, Charles and Myrtle White had previously owned the Tip Top Lunch in the Hollywood District of Salem during the early 1930s. When they moved their family to South Commercial Street in 1935, they built a new restaurant called White's Lunch on the property adjacent to their home. Myrtle and her son Robert ran the restaurant until she passed away in 1951, and then Robert and his brother Charles took it over. In 1952 the brothers assumed the business name of White's Lunch and Drive-In. In addition to advertising in the local paper for kitchen help and waitstaff, they sought "car hops." In 1955 Charles left the business, and Robert and his wife Carole became the sole owners.

Service and satisfaction were very important to the Whites, as stated on the cover of their early menus. They were originally open seventeen hours a day, from 8:00 a.m. to 1:00 a.m., seven days a week. A "plate lunch" special consisted of meat, two vegetables, bread, a beverage, and dessert for 35 cents.

Per White's, "Before there were skillets or scrambles there was Don's Big Mess. Bacon, sausage, ham, onions, bell peppers, mushrooms, tomatoes and hash browns grilled together and smothered in White's famous sausage gravy. Served with toast, biscuit or English muffin." While White's agreed to share what goes into Don's Big Mess, they aren't sharing the exact proportions or instructions for the recipe. This is a recipe I created based on the ingredients they shared with me.

SERVES 1–2

1 green bell pepper, diced

1 large tomato, diced

4 button mushrooms, sliced

1 onion, peeled and diced

4 slices bacon, chopped

½ cup diced ham

½ cup pork sausage

2 servings hash browns

Salt and pepper to taste

2 eggs, cooked to your preference and served on the side

Sausage gravy

1. Add everything except the eggs and sausage gravy to a large skillet and cook over medium-high heat until the sausage is no longer pink and the other ingredients are golden.

2. Place on a large plate and top with a cup of the sausage gravy.

SAUSAGE GRAVY
MAKES 2 CUPS

8 ounces pork sausage

3 tablespoons butter or margarine

1 clove garlic, minced

¼ cup flour

2⅓ cups milk

½ teaspoon salt

½ teaspoon pepper

⅛ teaspoon ground red pepper

1. Cook the sausage in a large skillet over medium heat, stirring until it crumbles and is no longer pink. Remove sausage and place on a paper towel.

2. Remove all the grease in the pan, except for 1 tablespoon.

3. Add the butter and garlic and cook until the butter melts.

4. Gently whisk in the flour and stir until smooth. Cook for about 1 minute, whisking constantly. Gradually stir in the milk and allow to cook, whisking constantly, for about 6 minutes or until thickened. Stir in sausage, salt, and pepper.

DOLLAR PANCAKES

1950, PICKET POST GUEST RANCH, SUPERIOR, ARIZONA

The Picket Post Guest Ranch started as the Picket Post Mansion that was the winter estate of Boyce Thompson Arboretum founder William Boyce Thompson. This "Castle on the Rocks" was built in phases between 1923 and 1929. The twenty-six-room mansion consisted of three separate structures partially built into the top of the crag. It included a two-story main house, an extant small residence for Thompson's wife Gertrude to the east, and Thompson's three-story private retreat called the Cliff House to the south. In 1928 Thompson donated the mansion and the surrounding property to the arboretum, but the maintenance costs proved too much, so the arboretum sold it in 1946.

In 1946 the new owners turned the house into the seasonal Picket House Guest Ranch and it was used as a lodge or inn. In 1950 the Picket Post Lodge Resort advertised super views of the desert and welcomed guests and diners from 8:00 a.m. to 11:00 p.m. They served a variety of meals, including these pancakes. They may no longer be in business, but you can sample this recipe from them.

SERVES ABOUT 4

1½ **cups bread flour**

1 **teaspoon salt**

1½ **teaspoons baking powder**

2 **eggs, lightly beaten**

1 **tablespoon butter, melted**

1 **teaspoon sugar or honey**

1¼ **cups milk**

1. Mix the dry ingredients together in a bowl.

2. Make a hole in the center of the flour mixture, then stir in the liquids and beat with a few swift strokes. Some lumps are okay. (Batter can be mixed and stored overnight in the refrigerator for use the next morning.)

3. Heat a griddle over medium-high heat. Lightly grease the griddle with butter and drop some batter onto the grill. The batter should be the size of a silver dollar.

4. The inn served their pancakes with a miniature jug of melted butter and warm mesquite honey.

STONE-GROUND MEAL PANCAKES

1946, THE COUNTRY STORE RESTAURANT, WESTON, VERMONT

In 1946 Vrest Orton and his wife Mildred opened a country store in a Victorian house along State Highway 100 in Weston, Vermont. Mildred not only managed the store finances but endeared herself to hungry customers. She offered ham sandwiches served on homemade stone-ground wheat bread baked in her own woodstove as well as country-style beans, pies, and cookies. She believed in wholesome eating and even published a recipe book in 1947 called *Cooking with Whole Grains*.

The restaurant was open seasonally from June to November, with diners enjoying a variety of items as they ate in the 1885-decorated dining room with its famous gold and mahogany antique soda fountain and a mahogany bar. Breakfast and lunch was served from 8:30 a.m. to 4:00 p.m. The *Ford Treasury Cookbook* noted, "Together the restaurant and the store, with its delightful and practical merchandise, are a museum of Americana." The Ortons also opened another store in Rockingham along State Highway 103 that was housed in a Victorian home with an 1871 covered bridge and overshot water wheel. While they no longer serve breakfast, you can still enjoy their stone-ground meal pancakes with this historic recipe.

SERVES 4–5

2 cups muffin meal*

5 teaspoons baking powder

¾ teaspoon salt

2 eggs, lightly beaten

1½ cups milk

3 tablespoons maple syrup or honey

¼ cup melted shortening or butter

1. Mix the dry ingredients together in a bowl, then add the liquids. Mix well, but do not overbeat. It's okay to have some lumps.

2. Heat a griddle over medium-high heat and drop tablespoons of batter on it. Allow to cook until bubbles appear and then flip and cook until golden or desired color.

3. Serve with Vermont maple syrup and Vermont country sausage.

Muffin meal is a blend of stone-ground corn, wheat, and rye.

CORNMEAL PANCAKES

1852, HOLBROOKE HOTEL, GRASS VALLEY, CALIFORNIA

The first building on this site was a miner's cabin built in 1850 by Charles L. Compton (a great-great uncle of this author), who was looking for gold. After that, the Golden Gate Saloon was built in 1852 by Stephen and Clara Smith, who were some of the first to invest in the boomtown known today as Grass Valley. A year later, the single-story Exchange Hotel, named for its convenience to the local Gold Exchange, was added behind the saloon. A fire in 1855 destroyed both, along with most of Grass Valley, but they were quickly rebuilt. After the fire, the owners quickly adapted and sold whiskey and beer to loyal customers from a tent among the rubble the next day. In 1862 the Exchange Hotel was caught in another blaze and was rebuilt as the two-story structure that remains to this day. To ensure another fire didn't destroy it, the building was fortified with heavy iron doors and a roof covered with twelve inches of dirt and brick. In 1878 W. C. Stokes was running the Exchange.

The current hotel's namesake, Daniel Holbrooke, was a native of Massachusetts and moved to California in 1849. He worked the mines during the Gold Rush and around 1852 built the English bridge that connected Grass Valley and Auburn. He then moved to Nevada City and then to Grass Valley, where he ran a wholesale and retail liquor business in 1867. He purchased the hotel in 1879 and called it the Holbrooke House. He and his wife Eleanor owned the business until his death in March 1883. Eleanor continued to manage and operate the hotel until her death in 1906.

Frank Dulmaine became the proprietor in August 1908 when he leased it from the executor of Eleanor Holbrooke's estate. Not long after taking over the Holbrooke, in October 1909, it was closed due to a gold strike. Yes, right in the middle of town! It seems the streets were being paved, and dirt from an old mine dump was used in the process. Once six "very handsome specimens" were picked up in a small radius, the road in front of the Holbrooke was closed when a rush of people hit the streets. Once the rush was over, the workers went back to the paving process. That December, Dulmaine hired Charles C. Marsh, who had just come from San Francisco, and he was well-known to prominent men as a "wiz" in cooking circles. He didn't stay long, and in 1910 Chef Yaheji "George" Hiramatsu was hired. The local paper reported, "Japanese chef George Hiramatsu will have each plate artistically ornamented." Despite his talent, he moved on and ended up in Idaho.

In December 1912 the hotel passed into the hands of Frank R. Hull and postmaster James C. Terrell from Frank Dulmaine, who was going into the mining business, which is where Hull came from. The owner of the building was Peter Johnson at the time. This was their first foray into the hotel and restaurant business, and they had several improvements in mind.

Hull managed the hotel and was assisted by his brother-in-law Samuel Culin. Terrell was, in essence, a silent partner and was not involved in the day-to-day operations. Hull hired German-native Chef Hans Von Bredow, who had come from San Francisco. His previous experience was with the Elks Club in San Mateo, where he gained the reputation of an outstanding chef. In 1915 the Holbrooke's menu included items like cream of celery soup, crab salad, baked halibut, Saratoga chips, corn on the cob, strawberry ice cream, iced watermelon, assorted cakes, and a variety of cheeses for after the meal.

In March of 1915, Hull hired Mr. and Mrs. Henry Mahr to manage the dining room for him. They had come from Imperial Valley, where Henry was working as a chef. For their April 1916 menu they offered fried salmon, roast turkey with dressing, peas, biscuits, fruit salad, pineapple ice cream, and homemade cookies. While they were serving good food, Mrs.

Mahr became ill and they left the Holbrooke and went back to San Francisco, and the dining room was closed until they could hire a new chef.

By March 1921, Hull turned the business over to L. B. Mason, who hired J. W. Glandon to be his dining room manager. Mason kept the business for two years and then sold the furnishings and lease to one-time Holbrooke clerk George Perkins. *The Morning Union* noted that "the Holbrooke is now under the management of George Perkins and he gives personal attention to his guests. There is nothing too good for the patrons of this well-known hotel." Perkins survived Prohibition by offering a "soft drink" bar and kept the hotel afloat until 1933, when he retired. The lease was sold to A. Vic McArthur and Dillard Reed, and Mrs. and Mrs. McArthur ran the hotel. Over the years, the hotel has had many owners and chefs, and they've been offering some of the same items for a long time, like these pancakes.

MAKES 2 DOZEN 5-INCH PANCAKES

2⅓ **cups flour**

2 **cups cornmeal**

2 **tablespoons sugar**

½ **teaspoon baking powder**

½ **teaspoon baking soda**

4 **eggs**

2¼ **cups buttermilk**

⅓ **cup butter, melted**

Piloncillo syrup

Agave butter

1. Combine the flour, cornmeal, sugar, baking powder, and baking soda in a bowl.

2. Whisk in the eggs and buttermilk and stir until just combined, then whisk in the melted butter. Set side.

3. Make the piloncillo syrup and agave butter and set aside.

4. To make the pancakes, scoop or ladle approximately ⅓ cup of batter onto a greased and preheated griddle. Cook until the sides are bubbly and the top is starting to look a little dry. Flip and continue to cook approximately 2 to 3 more minutes until cooked through.

5. Serve with piloncillo syrup and agave butter on the side.

PILONCILLO SYRUP
MAKES ½ CUP

1 **cone piloncillo sugar**

½ **cup water**

1. Combine the piloncillo and water in a saucepan and melt the sugar over medium heat.

2. Reduce until desired syrup consistency is reached. Keep warm until ready to serve.

AGAVE BUTTER
MAKES 2¼ CUPS

2 **cups butter, room temperature**

¼ **cup agave syrup**

Combine the butter with the agave syrup and blend well. Add more or less agave depending on the sweetness of butter desired.

BUTTERMILK PANCAKES

1885, LUTSEN RESORT, LUTSEN, MINNESOTA

George Nelson, son of Lutsen House owner C.A.A. Nelson and his wife Anna, met the love of his life when he was only thirteen years old during a berry-picking outing. His parents had invited their neighbors to pick blueberries with them when he first saw Inge Toftey. She was also thirteen, and George thought "Ingie" was the most beautiful girl on the North Shore. They married in May 1920. The couple lived on North Road in Lutsen for twenty-seven years and then spent their next forty-two in the apartment on the third floor of Lutsen Resort's main lodge. George passed away in 1993 at ninety-two, and a year later, Inga passed away at ninety-three. Inga developed many of the famed resort's recipes that are occasionally still served today. Her recipes include raisin-rye bread, white bread, and these buttermilk pancakes. For more history on Lutsen Resort, see the Swedish Meatballs recipe.

MAKES 12–15 3-INCH PANCAKES

2 eggs

2 cups buttermilk

1 cup flour

1½ tablespoons sugar

1 tablespoon salt

1 teaspoon baking soda

1 ounce melted butter

1. In a mixing bowl, combine the eggs and buttermilk and whisk until mixture is smooth.

2. Measure all the dry ingredients into a sifter and sift them into the eggs and milk. Whisk it all together to make sure it's smooth. Add the melted butter at the end, and whisk well one last time.

3. Pour 2 ounces of batter into a nonstick pan over medium heat. Flip the pancake once the bubbles pop and the outside starts to dry out.

4. Top with whipped cream, lingonberries, and maple syrup.

WAFFLES

1929, MILLER'S, RONKS, PENNSYLVANIA

For a detailed history of Miller's, see the Chicken and Waffles recipe, which these waffles pair with.

MAKES 7 WAFFLES USING A BELGIAN WAFFLE MAKER

2¼ cups flour

1 tablespoon baking powder

¼ cup granulated sugar

½ teaspoon kosher salt

2 large eggs, separated

½ cup vegetable oil

2 cups milk

2 teaspoons vanilla

1. Preheat a Belgian waffle iron and spray with nonstick cooking spray.

2. Whisk together the flour, baking powder, sugar, and salt in a large bowl.

3. In a separate medium-size bowl, beat the egg whites until stiff peaks form, but do not go further once they make stiff peaks or they will break. Set aside.

4. In a large measuring cup (or another medium-size bowl), whisk together the egg yolks, vegetable oil, milk, and vanilla.

5. Whisk the wet mixture into the dry ingredients and mix until most of the lumps are gone, and then gently fold in the egg whites with a rubber spatula.

6. Pour the batter into your waffle iron and cook according to the iron's directions.

Courtesy of Lancaster

7. Serve immediately with favorite toppings.

The amount of batter needed per waffle will depend on your waffle iron. My waffle iron uses just about a full cup of batter to make one waffle. To freeze, put the waffles on a baking sheet in one layer and place in the freezer until frozen, then store them in a freezer-safe zip-top bag for up to 3 to 4 weeks in the freezer. Reheat in a toaster or in a 350°F oven.

PARKER HOUSE ROLLS

1856, PARKER HOUSE, BOSTON, MASSACHUSETTS

The Parker House was founded by Harvey D. Parker, who was born in 1805 in Maine. According to the *Boston Sunday Globe* in 1881, when Parker set out for Boston in 1820, he carried a ten-dollar bill and a home-spun suit of clothes. His first job was that of a "chore boy" and then a coachman for a wealthy lady. While the lady was in town, Parker spent his time at a small eating house. He became acquainted with the owner, John E. Hunt, and eventually bought it from him for $432. His business outgrew the small building, so he opened Parker's Restaurant in Court Square in 1832, in the basement of the Tudor Building. In 1845 John F. Mills began working for Parker as a steward, and before leaving the Court Square location, Parker partnered with Mills and they formed Harvey D. Parker & Co. and hired James H. W. Huckins as their chef.

In 1854 Parker and Mills broke ground on School Street to build the Parker House. These men were the first to successfully establish a hotel on the European plan in Boston. Others had attempted, but failed. Chef James Huckins followed Parker to the new hotel, and an 1861 newspaper story noted that their grocery bill at Quincy Market was about $100,000 for meat and vegetables alone and the restaurant used 40,000 pounds of flour per month.

Parker employed a few chefs and cooks during his tenure, including James Huckins from the old location, but he left in 1864. Huckins was known for his soups while employed by Parker, and by 1868 his tomato soup was so popular that he sold the rights to the Boston Fruit Preserving Company, which canned it exclusively. The following year Parker House soups, salads, and dressings were being sold by Arthur H. Bailey & Co., who were general agents.

In 1864, after Huckins left, Augustine Anezin took over the head job. Anezin was a native of Marseilles, France, and was also the president of the newly formed Boston Culinary and Confectionery Society. He wasn't a newcomer to the scene—he previously had his own restaurant where Harvey Parker started out in Court Square, and prior to that he was the chef de cuisine at the Revere House for many years. Before joining Parker, Anezin announced that he and John Horan opened their restaurant at "Nos. 3 & 4 Court Square that was formerly occupied by Mr. H. D. Parker on May 12, 1862." That didn't last long, and a year later Anezin left the business to Horan. Anezin soon went back to the Parker House.

In 1875 Jean-Marie (Joseph) Brochen began working under Anezin and so did John Kraus, who was chef de confiserie, or head confectioner, from 1881 to 1884. When Anezin died in 1881, Brochen became the chef de cuisine and the vice president and, later, president of the Universal Union of Culinary Art in Boston. M. Louis Jaton was a chef under Brochen in 1883,

This was a 1935 birthday gathering for a New York City chef named "Papa Moneta" and Chef Bonello, seated on the right, attended.

and Henry Herding was the second cook under Brochen in 1884. Brochen remained the chef at the Parker House until his death in 1894.

The "famous Parker House rolls" were already being written about and a variety of recipes were shared in the local newspaper by 1868. In 1881 the Boston Cooking School was offering lessons on how to make Bavarian cream and Parker House rolls. They were *the* trendy bread in the 1800s, and bakeries and restaurants across the country started making and serving them.

The Parker House rolls' precise ingredients remained a well-kept secret until 1933, when Parker's head chef Giovanni "John" Bonello shared the recipe with Eleanor Roosevelt, who requested it. The story ran in the *Boston Herald* on March 24, 1933: "The secret of the Parker House rolls has been sent to Mrs. Franklin D. Roosevelt at the White House with the compliments of John Bonello, chef at the Boston hotel. 'This is the first time we have ever given out this recipe,' he wrote. 'So, Madam, you and the President may now enjoy them.'" The First Lady sent him a letter of thanks shortly thereafter, and the rest is tasty history!

MAKES 3 DOZEN ROLLS

½ **cup scalded milk**

½ **cup boiling water**

1 teaspoon salt

1 teaspoon sugar

1 tablespoon butter

½ **yeast cake dissolved in ¼ cup luke-warm water, or 2½ teaspoons instant yeast**

3 cups bread flour

Melted butter, for basting

1. Place the milk, water, salt, sugar, and butter into a mixing bowl and mix well.

2. Add the yeast, then add flour until it is stiff enough to knead. Let the dough rise in a warm place to double its bulk.

3. Preheat the oven to 400°F and line two baking sheets with parchment paper.

4. Scrape the dough out onto a lightly floured surface and shape it into a 9 x 16-inch rectangle. Using a floured knife, cut the dough lengthwise into 3 strips, then cut each strip crosswise into 12 small strips.

5. Working with one piece at a time, fold it unevenly so the top half slightly overlaps the bottom half. Tuck the over-hang under and place the roll seam side down on a baking sheet. Repeat with the remaining dough, forming 2 rows of 9 rolls on each baking sheet. Each roll should just touch, but leave about 4 inches between the rows.

6. Brush the rolls with butter and let them rise again, then bake for 15 minutes.

7. Brush the tops with butter again after baking.

SPOON BREAD

1926, THE WESTIN POINSETT HOTEL, GREENVILLE, SOUTH CAROLINA

This signature dish has been served at the Poinsett Hotel since 1926, and in 1948 the recipe was shared in a Greenville newspaper by the hotel's manager, J. Mason Alexander. His wife found the recipe in an old cookbook in 1926 and they started serving it with lunch and dinner. The recipe has changed a few times over the years and it's no longer served tableside for every meal. However, the current chef shared this recipe that he prepares upon request.

SERVES 12

4 tablespoons butter, divided

3 cups whole milk

1 cup cornmeal (white or yellow)

½ teaspoon salt

3 eggs, separated

¼ cup sugar

2 teaspoons baking powder

1. Preheat the oven to 375°F.

2. Butter a 5 x 9-inch glass dish with 1 tablespoon butter.

3. Heat the milk in a large saucepan until just simmering, then slowly whisk in the cornmeal and salt. Cook over low heat for 5 minutes.

4. Whisk the egg yolks and sugar together, then add to the cornmeal mixture to combine.

5. Remove the saucepan from the heat and add the remaining butter and baking powder. Stir to combine.

6. Whip the egg whites in a bowl until stiff peaks form and gently fold into the mixture.

7. Pour the batter into the buttered dish and bake for 20 to 25 minutes.

BAKING POWDER BISCUITS

1939, OLD HUNDRED, SOUTHBURY, CONNECTICUT

Baking powder biscuits are an old, classic recipe that require no yeast. Nellie I. Brown ran the Old Hundred inn and in 1939 she published a cookbook called *Recipes from Old Hundred: 200 Years of New England Cooking.* Recipes included dishes like Cranberry Muffins, Connecticut Fish Chowder, Veal Stew with Dumplings, Onion Shortcake, Old Hundred Cream Puffs, and Baking Powder Biscuits. This recipe can also accompany her Chicken Pie recipe found in the "Main Dishes" section.

MAKES 2 DOZEN BISCUITS

2 cups flour

1 teaspoon salt

4 teaspoons baking powder

3 tablespoons lard or cold butter

¾ cup milk

1. Sift the dry ingredients together in a bowl. Cut in the butter until the mixture is crumbly. Add the milk and mix well.

2. Knead the dough gently for about 30 seconds to combine.

3. Lightly dust a flat surface and pat the dough out with the palm of your hand until it is ¼-inch thick. This thickness will yield crispy biscuits, while leaving them ½-inch thick will make a softer dinner biscuit.

4. Cut the dough with a lightly floured biscuit cutter and place on a well-greased baking sheet.

5. Bake at 425°F for about 12 minutes or until golden brown.

These biscuits may be prepared an hour in advance, covered with wax paper, stored in the refrigerator, and baked when ready to serve.

JONNY CAKES

1755, KINGSTON INN, KINGSTON, RHODE ISLAND

Jonny cakes are a classic Colonial bread and nearly every inn offered their version. John Potter built an inn that was known alternatively as Barker's Tavern and the [Jesse] Babcock House. The tavern was later bought and run by Charles Barker from 1799 to 1819, and then Elisha Reynolds Potter Sr. bought it and operated it until his death in 1835. By 1875 it was run by J. S. Brown & Son and was officially known as the Kingston Inn.

SERVES 6–8

2 cups cornmeal

1 teaspoon salt

2 teaspoons sugar

3 cups boiling water

½ cup milk

1. Sift the cornmeal, salt, and sugar together in a bowl.

2. Gradually add the boiling water, stirring constantly, and then add the milk. Beat well.

3. Drop the batter on a hot griddle, well-greased with lard (or drippings or other fat), from a large tablespoon. Turn when golden brown, and be sure to keep the griddle well-greased.

4. Serve piping hot.

DATE NUT BREAD

1940s, THE INN AT DEATH VALLEY, DEATH VALLEY, CALIFORNIA

It was in 1883 when William Coleman built Greenland Ranch because of the natural springs around it. The Harmony Borax Works housed the miners and freighters there who hauled the borax out of the valley. Coleman raised cattle and grew melons, sweet potatoes, and tomatoes, while others had vegetable patches and fruit trees like oranges and dates.

The Furnace Creek Ranch (now the Inn at Death Valley) was built in 1927 on the site of Greenland Ranch and was managed by Beulah Brown. It was a working ranch with Hereford cows, alfalfa, kafir corn, wheat, oats, oranges, and vegetables. But most interesting were the date palm trees. *The Chronicle* in Leavenworth, Kansas, wrote, "Most interesting, however, are the young Deglet Noir date palms, of which there are 126, some placed by the government in the hope of obtaining pest-free nursery stock." Date palms still surround the Inn at Death Valley and are used in many of their recipes.

In 1929 Kathryn Ronan from Ireland managed the inn, and she employed cooks Lee Na Sing and Lee I Jor in 1930 and then in 1940 hired Gayle Rainsdall as chef and Oscar Haggard to be the baker. In 1958 James "Jim" Marquez was the chef and he created this signature recipe for the inn. He used dates from the date palm orchard at the inn and started serving it to the guests for breakfast and in picnic lunches. By 1973 they had baked and served 100,000 loaves of the bread.

MAKES 1 LOAF

½ **cup white sugar**

½ **cup brown sugar**

1 **teaspoon baking soda**

1 **teaspoon salt**

4 **tablespoons butter**

1 **cup water**

½ **pound pitted and chopped dates**

1½ **cups flour**

½ **cup chopped walnuts**

1. Preheat the oven to 325°F.

2. Cream the sugars, baking soda, and salt with the butter until light and fluffy.

3. Add the water and dates, and mix well. Add the flour and mix for 1 minute, then add the walnuts.

4. Pour the batter into a greased and lined 9 x 5-inch bread tin. Bake for 45 minutes or until a toothpick comes out clean.

PUMPKIN BREAD

1796, FITZWILLIAM INN, FITZWILLIAM, NEW HAMPSHIRE

The town of Fitzwilliam was founded in 1764 and by the turn of the nineteenth century it was a thriving, self-sufficient community that was surrounded by farms, while boasting of several dozen local businesses. The women and men of that bygone era lived off the fruits of the earth, producing their own livestock and fresh fruits and vegetables, and shared music and dance with their neighbors in the community.

The Fitzwilliam Inn, which sits in the shadow of Mount Monadnock, was built in 1796 as a stop on the old coach road between Boston and points north. The inn was a spot where people would come to meet, share, and celebrate. In 1837 Mr. J. Reed was running the Fitzwilliam Hotel, as it was called during his tenure, and then by June 1838 it was kept by Colonel William Lebourveau and was also known as Lebourveau's Tavern. He kept the hotel, which was and still is opened seasonally, until 1862.

From 1863 to 1880 Abner Gage ran the hotel, which was also referred to as Gage's Hotel. During his time at the hotel, he often sought reliable help. In 1869 Gage advertised that he was looking for "a man and wife without incumberance [sic], to work in a hotel; the wife to cook and the man to work in the stable, etc. They must be sober, honest, and industrious people. Wages $30 per month." He took out a similar ad in 1872 and wanted "an American man and wife to work in a hotel. The wife to cook, the man to do the stable work, drive to the Depot with express mail and be a live man. To the right persons I will pay $500 a year, and if they don't swear or use tobacco, I will pay $25 more. (We don't keep whiskey.)" Gage died in September 1881 and by 1884 Perry & Atkinson and then J. L. Perry took over. By the turn of the century, the inn was being called the Fitzwilliam Tavern and sometimes the Fitzwilliam Hotel.

Around 1920 and until 1938, John Blair ran it by the name Fitzwilliam Tavern. But by 1946 George Francis and Katharine Whitcomb were managing the place, now being called an inn again, and did so for ten years or so before retiring. It changed hands a few more times after that, and in the 1970s and '80s it was owned by opera star Barbara Wallace and her husband, Charlie. It's still open seasonally, but you can enjoy their popular pumpkin bread anytime. It's been a hit at the inn since at least the 1960s.

MAKES 1 LOAF

2 eggs

1 cup sugar

⅓ cup oil

⅔ cup pumpkin

¼ cup water

1⅓ cups flour

½ teaspoon baking soda

¼ teaspoon baking powder

¼ teaspoon salt

¼ teaspoon cinnamon

¼ teaspoon nutmeg

1. Preheat the oven to 350°F.

2. Beat the eggs in a large bowl until blended. Add the sugar, oil, pumpkin, and water and mix.

3. Sift the remaining ingredients together in a small bowl. Add to the wet mixture and beat well. Pour into a greased 8½ x 4½-inch loaf pan.

4. Bake for about 1 hour or until a toothpick comes out clean.

5. Cool on rack for 10 minutes. Remove from the pan and allow to cool on a cake rack.

HUCKLEBERRY MUFFINS

1886, CRESCENT HOTEL & SPA,
EUREKA SPRINGS, ARKANSAS

The Crescent Hotel opened in 1886 high atop a mountain and was hand-constructed of Arkansas limestone by Irish stonemasons at a cost of $284,000. The five-story castle's stonemasons cut and stacked eighteen-inch-thick limestone blocks that were quarried about ten miles away near the White River and brought to the site by horse-drawn wagons. The *Eureka Springs Times Echo* reported on the grand opening on May 20, 1886: "With the opening of the grandiose Crescent Hotel, Eureka Springs entered a new and exciting era. Notables from afar are arriving in our fair city and soon many others will follow. The Crescent, built by the Eureka Springs Improvement Company and The Frisco Railroad is America's most luxurious resort hotel. Featuring large airy rooms, comfortably furnished, the Crescent Hotel offers the visiting vacationer opulence unmatched in convenience and service. Tonight's gala ball will find in attendance many of the leaders in business and society. As guest of honor, the Honorable James G. Blaine, the Republican presidential nominee, will attend with his charming wife Laura. The very popular Harry Barton and his orchestra will play for tonight's festivities. In the Grand Ballroom of the new Crescent, the opening banquet for the 400 celebrants will be followed by a dedication ceremony where the honorable Mr. Blaine will be the guest speaker. His introduction by Mr. Powell Clayton will follow an invocation by Reverend McElwee."

The Crescent was opened to welcome health-seekers to the numerous springs nearby. These tasty treasures have been served for decades at the hotel that sits atop the crest of the Ozark mountains surrounded by the hilly town of Eureka Springs.

MAKES ABOUT 8 MUFFINS

2 cups flour

4 teaspoons baking powder

⅓ cup shortening

1 cup milk

1 egg, beaten

1 cup huckleberries, washed and drained, mixed with ½ teaspoon flour (blueberries can be substituted)

1. Preheat the oven to 350°F.

2. Sift the dry ingredients and cut in the shortening. To this add the milk and beaten egg. Stir the floured berries in quickly, but don't mash them.

3. Bake in a hot greased muffin pan for 20 minutes.

VANILLA MUFFINS

1869, THE PEABODY, MEMPHIS, TENNESSEE

The recipe for vanilla muffins at the Peabody dates back decades. No one knows exactly when they first appeared, but by 1928 they were so popular that the *Boston Herald* and other newspapers published the recipe. According to the story, Gilbert Blanc, the chef at the time, stated, "My favorite recipe is really two—both of which I picked up from an old negro plantation cook." The paper also reported that the muffins were so well liked that they were shipped all over the country. The muffins were "made famous by the Peabody" according to the *Jackson Sun* newspaper ten years later. When Marilyn Belz (of the Belz family that many decades later came to own the hotel) and her friends would stop in for a bite after dancing the night away to one of the big band orchestras in the Peabody Skyway, the vanilla muffins were what was served as a late-night snack. Today the vanilla muffins are still sold as a popular breakfast item at Peabody Deli & Desserts, and they are an after-dinner "take-home" at Chez Philippe and frequently sent to guests and clients as a treat. This is Chef Gilbert Blanc's 1928 recipe.

MAKES 26 MUFFINS

4 eggs

2 cups sugar

4 cups flour

1 tablespoon baking powder

1 stick (½ cup) butter, melted

2 cups milk

1 tablespoon vanilla

1. Preheat the oven to 350°F.

2. In a large bowl, combine the eggs and sugar and then add the flour and baking powder.

3. Add the butter and stir. Stir in the milk and vanilla and mix until all the ingredients are incorporated, but do not overbeat.

4. Grease or line a muffin pan and bake for 15 to 20 minutes or until a toothpick comes out clean.

MAPLE MUFFINS

1920, MAPLE CABIN, ST. JOHNSBURY, VERMONT

Breakfast & Luncheons
8 until 4

the Maple Cabin

PORTLAND STREET
Next to Cary Maple Factory

The Maple Cabin tearoom was opened in 1920 by the George C. Cary Co. on Portland Street. The *St. Johnsbury Republican* reported on the opening: "Keep your eye on Maple Town! It is a new name applied to an old section of the town." They went on to describe the cabin: "Going through the door of this attractive log cabin one enters a large square room attractively decorated. Opposite the large door is a large brick fireplace with blazing maple log. On the walls are paddles, birch bark canoe and hatchet, remainders of the Indians who discovered maple. The room is furnished with brown wicker furniture and flower boxes containing blue lobelias, blue curtains and hangings carry out the color scheme of Belgian blue and white. In the cabin lunches and ice cream are served and all varieties of Maple Grove candies and Vermont maple sugar and syrup are for sale as well as homemade cakes and cookies."

Cary's cabin was built adjacent to the maple sugar factory and became a popular destination. The company hired three young ladies, Gertrude Franklin, Essie Sylvester, and Mrs. Morris Seales, to run the cabin. In 1922 the inn still employed Miss Franklin, who was joined by George Cary's daughter, Madeline. By 1928 Cary's sister, Mrs. Josephine Cary Smith, was the manager and hostess of the cabin. Two years later the Maple Cabin Inn was opened across from the cabin itself to accommodate people coming to the area. The *Fairbanks Centennial* reported, "The Maple Cabin which has become a favorite of many St. Johnsbury people, continues this summer to serve the chicken and waffles for which it has become famous, as well as delicious soups, salads, home-made cakes, ice creams, and other specialties."

George Cary, the founder of the cabin and the Cary Maple Sugar Candy Company, died in 1931. At that time, he was dubbed "the maple sugar king." It was 1939 when his sister Josephine announced she was closing the cabin as of December 15 and leaving for Los Angeles. Almost a year to the day, she passed away in that city after battling a two-year illness. On June 12, 1948, Mr. and Mrs. James Willey reopened the cabin that was now next door to the Cary Maple Sugar Company. Like before, it served breakfast and lunch and offered sandwiches as well as an assortment of maple sugar products. A year later, the Boylan sisters, Patricia and Ann, became the new managers and continued to offer specialty maples items like syrup and candies. In 1952, the Maple Cabin was turned into a museum by the Cary Maple Sugar Company. Its kitchen housed a miniature movie theater, and the main building housed the company's consumer products. Today it's a private residence.

MAKES 8 MUFFINS

1 egg

¼ cup milk

1¾ cups flour

2½ teaspoons baking powder

¼ teaspoon salt

½ cup maple syrup

¼ cup melted butter

1. Beat the egg in a large bowl and then add the milk. Beat until well-blended.

2. Sift the flour, baking powder, and salt together in a small bowl.

3. Gradually add the flour to the egg and milk mixture, alternating with the maple syrup. Fold the melted butter into the mixture.

4. Bake in a buttered and floured muffin tin at 325°F for about 25 minutes.

BREAKFAST RIDE POTATOES

1965, WHITE STALLION RANCH, TUCSON, ARIZONA

The True family has been operating the White Stallion Ranch since 1965, but the property's history is much older than that. The ranch was originally built in the early 1900s and started as a cattle ranch that was constructed of Mexican adobe, which is brick made of mud and straw. During a later renovation, wire and horseshoes were found in the walls.

It was homesteaded by David Young from 1936 to 1939, and he was the first deeded owner of the property. After that, Herbert and Vine Bruning purchased the property and used it as a ranch where they raised cattle, chickens, and turkeys. They changed the name to CB Bar Ranch, and it was home to 30,000 birds. In 1945 Max Zimmerman, a Chicago liquor store owner, bought the ranch and moved West. Zimmerman named it the MZ Bar Ranch and turned it into a guest ranch. He constructed six buildings complete with kitchenettes for guests, and those buildings are still standing, but several renovations later they no longer resemble the original guest room interiors. In 1949 Mary Varner bought the property and continued to operate it as a guest ranch and also offered long-term rentals to the nearby Marana Army Airfield. Years later, Brew and Marge Towne, of Cape Cod, Massachusetts, fulfilled their dream of owning a guest ranch and named it the White Stallion. They really wanted to name it the Black Stallion, but reconsidered when they realized that "BS Ranch" wasn't such a great idea.

It was 1965 when Allen and Cynthia True came from Colorado to make the ranch their home. Along with them were their sons, Russell, who was just five years old, and Michael, who was still in a crib. At the time, the ranch consisted of seventeen rooms, seventeen horses, and 200 acres. The number of guest ranches left in the area had dropped to about thirty, so Allen and Cynthia began purchasing adjacent land as it became available, which increased the ranch to 3,000 acres. The ranch serves up three squares a day, but for those heading out for an early morning ride, these signature potatoes are served. They're cooked the same way they have been for fifty-plus years, which is out in the desert in the same cast-iron pans over an open fire. According to the ranch, "We use leftover baked potatoes and use up potatoes from dinners."

8 cups boiled potatoes, cut into thumb-size pieces

2½ tablespoons onion salt

1¾ teaspoons black pepper

⅔ cup paprika

1 cup cooked crumbled bacon

2–4 tablespoons olive oil

1. Combine the seasonings and toss with the potatoes. Add the bacon and mix together.

2. Heat the olive oil in a large pan over medium-high heat. Fry the potatoes until hot, then place in a large bowl and serve.

APPETIZERS, SOUPS, and SALADS

OYSTERS ROCKEFELLER & BIENVILLE

1840, ANTOINE'S, NEW ORLEANS, LOUISIANA

Antoine's restaurant was opened by Antoine Alciatore in 1840 in the French Quarter on St. Louis Street. He was born in Alassio, Italy, on December 18, 1822, but his family soon moved to Marseilles, France. He emigrated to America around 1839 and arrived in New York City. He made his way to the bustling city of New Orleans, where he briefly worked in the kitchen of the grand St. Charles Hotel.

By the 1840s Antoine had opened a *pension,* which is a place to sleep and eat, on St. Louis Street. He felt at home in the French-speaking city of New Orleans, where aristocrats with extravagant palates were an ideal audience for his culinary artistry. His *pension* eventually turned into a full restaurant where his culinary genius was enjoyed by many. An 1866 ad in the *Weekly Iberville South* newspaper read "Restaurant Antoine. Tenu Par Antoine Alciator. 50 Rue St. Louis." The ad also included (translated) "Between the passage of the stock exchange and the Rue Royale. Salon for Wedding and Meals of Families. Rooms stocked for inhabitants."

Antoine created wonderful meals for the people of New Orleans for decades, and some of his family worked for him, too. Sadly, he became ill in the 1870s and went to France to live out his days as his life was nearing its end. He also wanted to die and be buried in France. According to the family, he told his wife Julie that he did not want her to watch him deteriorate and said as he left, "As I take a boat for Marseilles, we will not meet again on Earth." He died in Marseilles on August 20, 1877.

Antoine left Julie in charge, and their son Jules apprenticed under his mother. Jules was sent to France to hone his culinary skills and returned to America a classically trained French chef. He worked at the Pickwick Club until 1887 and then returned to Antoine's. Jules, like his father, was an excellent chef and created the restaurant's signature Oysters Rockefeller. According to the family, Jules created the now-famous dish in the 1890s when he couldn't get snails. New Orleans had a bounty of oysters, so he substituted them for his creation.

A quick search of old cookbooks and newspapers shows just how many people have tried to re-create this recipe. The family told me this: "The original recipe included forty pounds of butter. He named it Rockefeller because the dish was rich and he was the richest man in the world at the time." They also told me that the recipe does not include bacon, spinach, or nuts, but it does include herbs, hollandaise sauce, greenery, and spices. On top of that, they shared that it's not just the ingredients, but the secret is in the preparation of the ingredients.

Of course, they are not sharing their signature recipe and I respect that, nor am I going to attempt to create one. Honestly, as they told me, "Only about five people know the recipe. The fact that the recipe remains a closely guarded secret in this technological and social media world is an amazing feat and keeps the mystery and mystique of the legacy alive." We both want you to taste some of Antoine's amazing history, so they shared their signature Oysters Bienville recipe with me.

MAKES 3 DOZEN

4 tablespoons butter

1½ cups minced green pepper

1 cup minced green onion

2 garlic cloves, minced

½ cup white wine

½ cup chopped pimento

1½ cups béchamel sauce

⅔ cup grated Romano cheese

½ cup bread crumbs

Salt and white pepper

3 dozen raw oysters on the half shell

1. Melt the butter and sauté the peppers, onions, and garlic until limp. Add the wine and bring to a boil.

2. Add the pimento, béchamel, grated cheese, bread crumbs, and salt and white pepper to taste. Simmer for 15 minutes, stirring occasionally. Set aside.

3. Place the oysters on a baking sheet and cover each one with the béchamel sauce. Bake for 8 to 10 minutes in a 400°F oven until the sauce is lightly browned.

BÉCHAMEL SAUCE
MAKES 1½ CUPS

2 tablespoons butter

2 tablespoons flour

1½ cups milk

Salt and white pepper to taste

Melt the butter in a small saucepan over medium to high heat and whisk in flour until it becomes foamy. Whisk in the milk, bring to a boil, and then turn down heat to a simmer. Add salt and white pepper to taste and remove from heat.

SHRIMP COCKTAIL

1902, ST. ELMO STEAK HOUSE, INDIANAPOLIS, INDIANA

St. Elmo Steak House has been a landmark in downtown Indianapolis since 1902. It was founded by Joe Stahr, who named the restaurant after the patron saint of sailors, St. Elmo. Starting out with a beautiful tiger-oak back bar purchased in Chicago, the restaurant was simply a small tavern with a basic menu. Through the years, its classic turn-of-the-century Chicago saloon decor has changed very little, beyond the inevitable expansions. In 1914 the restaurant hired Karl Burch as a waiter and he worked there for fifty-four years and retired at the age of eighty-nine!

One of their signature items is the shrimp cocktail, and Joe was known for his. In fact, when he was preparing to retire from the business in 1946, the local paper wrote this about him: "Mr. Stahr has a way with shrimp and his shrimp dishes, especially his shrimp cocktails, always have been in great demand." In 1947 St. Elmo's cocktail included three shrimp with cocktail sauce and cost thirty cents.

It's not surprising that the precursor to the shrimp cocktail was the oyster cocktail, since oysters were wildly popular in the 1800s and shrimp were not. The oyster cocktail was created by German immigrant A. Louis "George" Thiele in San Francisco in 1868. He even applied for a patent, and the paper claims it was granted to him by October 1868. Thiele owned the Faust Cellar Beer and Billiard Saloon on Clay and Montgomery Streets. The oyster cocktail was considered a drink well into the 1800s and variations of the recipe included oysters, oyster liquor, lemon juice, tomato sauce, Worcestershire sauce, Tabasco sauce, or horseradish.

As early as the 1890s, Texas was advertising fried shrimp with cocktail sauce and shrimp cocktails. After the turn of the century, the appetizer started appearing in various states across the country, including Wisconsin, Kentucky, New Jersey, New York, Kansas, Pennsylvania, Alabama, and Indiana. Joe Stahr enjoyed feeding people in Indianapolis well, and he served both oyster and shrimp cocktails. The secret to their dish is the immense amount of horseradish they use in it. Trust me, I've tried it, and I still remember the vapor-lock like it was yesterday!

A vintage photo of Joe Stahr in the bar with a sign behind him that shows: "Shrimp Cocktail for $.10"

MAKES 1 COCKTAIL

4 large raw shrimp

St. Elmo cocktail sauce

1. Fill a pot with 4 quarts of water and bring to a rolling boil. (It's important to use a full 4 quarts for this step.)

2. Fill a medium-size bowl with 4 cups of ice and 1 cup of water.

3. Set a timer for 2 minutes and 15 seconds.

4. Carefully put the shrimp in the boiling water and remove from heat.

5. Start the timer. Stir the shrimp.

6. When the time is up, immediately remove the shrimp with a slotted spoon and place into the bowl of ice water. Toss the shrimp in the ice water for 3 minutes or until completely chilled.

7. Serve with cocktail sauce. Note, their signature cocktail sauce is really hot and a pale pink color.

Shrimp may be stored in a sealed container in the refrigerator for up to two days.

PICKLED SHRIMP

1947, VILLULA TEA GARDEN, SEALE, ALABAMA

The Villula Tea Garden was a charming Southern restaurant operated by Helen Joerg, who believed customers should be treated like family. In 1978 Columbus, Georgia's *Ledger-Enquirer* wrote a story about Helen, who was eighty-three at the time and still working. She recalled, "Sometimes on a Sunday the room will be full. There'll be people here from seven different communities, and I'll know everyone in the room." She also said, "You know, that's really the thing about it—It makes you feel good to have pleased somebody."

Helen Joerg in her Vilulla Tea Garden, 1960.

Customers came for Helen's delicious Southern food and also shopped at her gift shop that sold home decor and had an atmosphere of what she called her "tea room." Customers sat in woven cane chairs, and the dining area included a fireplace and wooden floors that made people feel like they were dining in her home. Helen shared, "Tea rooms are practically extinct now, you know. Everything's commercial these days. I don't know of any other tea room. We lose money every month, but I love it. I love the folks who come here. Of course, I've had to slow down as far as staying open too much at night, but we're now open only for lunch every day and at night by appointment." This was one of her signature dishes.

SERVES 20

2½ pounds shrimp

6 celery tops

3½ teaspoons salt

¼ cup mixed pickling spice

1 cup peeled and sliced onions

7–8 bay leaves

1¼ cups salad oil

¾ cup vinegar

2 teaspoons salt

½ teaspoon celery seed

2½ tablespoons capers with juice

Dash of Tabasco sauce

1. Place the shrimp in a pot and cover with water. Add the celery tops, salt, and pickling spice. Cook for about 10 minutes over high heat or until the shrimp is pink.

2. Drain the shrimp and rinse with cold water. Peel the shrimp.

3. Layer the shrimp and onions in a shallow glass dish and add bay leaves.

4. Combine the oil, vinegar, salt, celery seed, capers, and hot sauce and mix well.

5. Pour the marinade over the shrimp and onions and cover. Marinate for at least 24 hours or up to 1 week.

CRAB IMPERIAL
SCOTCH EGG

1816, INN AT PERRY CABIN, ST. MICHAELS, MARYLAND

Samuel Hambleton constructed his home and farm around 1815 after Congress awarded him a small land grant in St. Michaels, Maryland, where he had grown up as a child. Hambleton developed a tobacco farm of nearly two dozen acres that he called Navy Point. He retired to St. Michaels in 1816 and designed the north wing, which is approximately where the Morning Room is. At its center was a stunning Greek Revival–style manor that he had named Perry Cabin after his longtime friend Commodore Oliver Hazard Perry. In fact, most of the building's interior spaces resembled the living quarters that the commodore inhabited on board his second flagship, the USS *Niagara*. Upon Hambleton's death in 1851, the entire estate continued to serve as a farm for nearly a hundred years.

In approximately 1926, coal baron Charles Fogg owned Perry Cabin and drastically renovated the manor house to the then-fashionable Federal and Greek Revival architectural styles, including the columned portico on the front entrance facing the harbor. In 1952 the Watkins family transformed the location into a prominent riding academy. Its transformation exposed it to a wealth of new people in the equine racing community, including Harry and Teresa Meyerhoff, who owned the 1979 Kentucky Derby winner, Spectacular Bid. Upon discovering the manor and falling in love with the area, they bought it in 1980 and renovated it into a small holiday destination called the Inn at Perry Cabin. Initially numbering just six rooms, it quickly grew in size once Sir Bernard Ashley acquired it nearly a decade later. Over the years the Inn at Perry Cabin evolved into a leading destination resort known the world over. In 1999 it was sold to Orient-Express Hotels, which continued with ongoing renovations.

Crab was, and still is, a popular menu item in St. Michaels and at the Inn at Perry Cabin. In 1950 Mr. and Mrs. Robert Hunteman owned the farm and held a crab fest at their home for a local nonprofit. The inn has been serving crab imperial since the 1980s. This recipe is from Chef Gregory James, who loves reading old cookbooks but stays in tune with trends. He sources his products, like seafood, meat, and produce, from local fishermen and farmers as often as possible. He also has his own garden and beehives and brews beer, makes cheese and ice cream, and cans food as well. Chef says, "I love having the freedom to create recipes using our immense local bounty."

SERVES 6

2 cups spinach, blanched and drained

6 six-minute (soft-boiled) eggs, peeled

Crab Imperial Mix (recipe follows)

⅓ cup flour

3 eggs, beaten, for egg wash

1 cup panko bread crumbs

Oil, for frying

1¼ teaspoons Old Bay Seasoning

Imperial Sauce (recipe follows)

1. Divide the blanched spinach into 6 piles. Wrap the spinach leaves around each of eggs until they are completely encased, then wrap each of the eggs with Imperial Mix. Refrigerate for 30 minutes to firm up.

2. Gently flour the wrapped eggs, then dip them into the egg wash and finally the panko bread crumbs. Refrigerate and allow to rest again for 1 hour.

3. Heat the oil in a tall saucepan over medium-high heat to 325°F.

4. Cook the eggs until golden brown. Remove from oil, place onto a clean cutting board, and dry on a paper towel.

5. Slice the eggs in half, lengthwise. Place ⅓ cup of Imperial Sauce on each plate and place two egg halves on top. Season with Old Bay.

CRAB IMPERIAL MIX
MAKES ABOUT 2 CUPS

¼ cup Duke's mayonnaise

1¾ teaspoons Dijon mustard

1 teaspoon Worcestershire sauce

1 teaspoon hot chili sauce

1 egg yolk

Zest from ½ lemon

¾ teaspoon Old Bay Seasoning

¾ teaspoon chopped parsley

¾ teaspoon minced chives

1½ cups lump crabmeat

1. In a small bowl, combine all the ingredients and mix well.

2. Transfer to a sheet pan, plate, or flat surface, and leave out or refrigerate to allow the mix to "dry out."

IMPERIAL SAUCE
MAKES 2 CUPS

⅓ cup Duke's mayonnaise

1¾ teaspoons Dijon mustard

1½ teaspoons Worcestershire sauce

1½ teaspoons IPC Fresno chili sauce

1 egg yolk

Zest from ½ lemon

¾ teaspoon chopped parsley

¾ teaspoon minced chives

1. In a small bowl, combine all the ingredients and mix well.

2. Transfer to a pint container and refrigerate until ready to serve.

OLD BAY SEASONING 1940S

Just about everyone on the Eastern Shore grew up with Old Bay Seasoning. It was originally called Delicious Brand Shrimp and Crab Seasoning, and its creator was merchant Gustav Brunn, who narrowly escaped Nazi Germany and sailed to the United States in 1939. Brunn ended up in Baltimore with his small spice grinder that he brought with him. He combined eighteen spices and herbs to make the now-renowned recipe. He later named the seasoning after a steamship line that traveled the Chesapeake between Maryland and Virginia. Chefs and home cooks have been using it ever since.

CANINE ROCKFISH

1816, INN AT PERRY CABIN, ST. MICHAELS, MARYLAND

Chef Gregory James prides himself on making just about everything from scratch and using as many local ingredients as he can. When his dog Bronson, who was seventeen, started to develop food allergies, he decided to create some recipes for him. That led him to offer "menu items" for the inn's furry guests, who are as pampered as the human ones. For the history of the Inn at Perry Cabin, see the Crab Imperial Scotch Egg recipe.

SERVES YOUR CANINE FRIEND AS NEEDED

1½ pounds rockfish fillets

1 cup uncooked brown rice

2 cups vegetable broth

¾ cup chopped fresh broccoli

1 cup chopped zucchini

1 cup chopped sweet potatoes

1 cup fresh spinach

1. Place all the ingredients in a slow cooker in the order listed, covering the rockfish completely with vegetables. Cook 1 hour on high or 2 hours on low.

2. Remove the rockfish from the slow cooker, shred it, and then return it to the rice and veggie mixture, stirring until evenly distributed.

3. Store covered in the fridge for up to 3 days or freeze in single-serve portions.

HUSKY KING CRAB BOAT

1960, FAIRBANKS INN, FAIRBANKS, ALASKA

The Fairbanks Inn opened in 1960 at 1521 Cushman in downtown Fairbanks and offered informal luxury for guests as they enjoyed breakfast, lunch, or dinner. In 1963 manager Kenneth Friske knew an expansion was needed to support the increasing number of tourists, so they set out to add additional capacity that was projected to cost $1 million. The Fairbanks Inn was the first in town to offer a TV in each room, an outdoor recreation area, and an automatic guest-style phone system message service. The renovation also included a dining room and cocktail lounge that in 1964 started offering whole live New England lobsters.

A year later the *Sunday World-Herald* in Omaha, Nebraska, reported, "On registered at the Fairbanks Inn, to find yourself in a world of sanitized toilet seats, free TV, multilingual chambermaids, and a cuisine that embraces filet mignon and Eskimo-caught shee-fish." The inn is no longer in business.

SERVES 4

1 green pepper, diced

1½ teaspoons diced onion

5 tablespoons sherry wine

3½ tablespoons diced pimento

2 cups warm white sauce (see recipe for béchamel on page 33)

1 pound Alaskan king crabmeat

2 cups whipped mashed potatoes

4 hard-boiled eggs, shredded

1. Simmer the green pepper and onion in the sherry over low heat until tender. Drain and add them, along with the pimento, to the warm white sauce.

2. Heat the crab in salted simmering water.

3. While the crab is warming up, prepare four small oval casserole dishes by piping potato rosettes (or you can scoop them) at the end of each casserole as you like.

4. Place ½ cup of the sauce in each casserole. Drain the crabmeat and place equal portions on the sauce.

5. Sprinkle each serving with the shredded eggs and serve.

CHILES RELLENOS

1926, LA FONDA HOTEL, SANTA FE, NEW MEXICO

According to La Fonda's history, the city records show the existing building sits on the site of the town's first inn that was established when Santa Fe was founded in 1607 by Spaniards. In 1821 Captain William Becknell and his party found their way to La Fonda during the maiden commercial route across the plains from Missouri, establishing the Santa Fe Trail as well as La Fonda's reputation for hospitality. Throughout the nineteenth century, La Fonda quickly became the preferred lodging option among trappers, soldiers, gold seekers, gamblers, and politicians.

The structure that guests enjoy today was built in 1922 and features the influence of architects Mary Elizabeth Jane Colter and John Gaw Meem. Authentic elements including hand-carved beams, stained glass skylights, and a twenty-five-foot cathedral ceiling create a romantic aura unique to La Fonda's Santa Fe history. Elements of the original design are still evident throughout the hotel, with the restaurant La Plazuela situated on the hotel's original 1920s outdoor patio, as well as breathtaking skylights, terra-cotta tile, and hammered tin chandeliers in the event venues. In 1925 the building changed hands again when it was acquired by the Atchison, Topeka & Santa Fe Railway. The company leased the property to Fred Harvey, a gentleman renowned for his keen sense of hospitality. Harvey introduced his own personal touch and made the inn a Harvey House. Harvey Houses were known for their high standards, fine dining, and the signature Harvey Girls that were a staff of exceptionally well-trained single waitresses. La Fonda has been offering chiles rellenos since 1926. This is their current version from Chef Lane Warner.

SERVES 4-8

8 ounces Chihuahua cheese

8 ounces Asadero cheese

½ cup half-and-half

8 Hatch green chiles, roasted and peeled (remove seeds for less heat)

7½ ounces flour

1 tablespoon baking powder

½ tablespoon sugar

½ tablespoon salt

1 teaspoon white pepper

1 teaspoon paprika

12 ounces beer

1 egg yolk

24 ounces peanut oil, for frying

1. Mix the cheeses and half-and-half until smooth and creamy. Place in a pastry bag and fill the chiles.

2. For the batter, mix the dry ingredients together, add the beer and egg yolk, and mix until smooth.

3. Lightly coat the stuffed rellenos with batter and fry at 300°F until golden brown.

4. Serve with your favorite red or green chile, topped with Chihuahua cheese and melted.

BUFFALO WINGS

1964, ANCHOR BAR, BUFFALO, NEW YORK

According to the Anchor Bar, buffalo wings were "invented" on a Friday night in 1964 by Dominic Bellissimo's mother, Teressa. He was tending bar at the Anchor when late that evening, a group of his friends arrived with ravenous appetites. Dominic asked his mother to prepare something for his friends to eat. Being a good Italian mom, she obliged and went to the kitchen where she found some chicken wings that were reserved for making soup stock. Teressa deep-fried the wings and flavored them with a sauce she whipped up with ingredients at hand. The wings were an instant hit and it didn't take long for people to flock to the bar to experience this new taste sensation.

The phenomenon created in 1964 by Teressa Bellissimo has since spread across the globe. Although many have tried to duplicate Anchor's buffalo wings, the closely guarded secret recipe is what makes their version the proclaimed "Best Wings in the World."

MAKES 12–16 WINGS

12–16 chicken wings

½ cup Anchor Bar's Original Medium Sauce*

1. Pat the wings dry, splitting them at the joint if desired.

2. Deep-fry at 350°F for 10 to 12 minutes or bake at 425°F for 45 minutes until cooked through and crispy.

3. Drain the wings and put them in a large bowl. Add the sauce and toss until the wings are completely coated. Serve with blue cheese and celery.

You might be able to get the sauce from your grocery store or you can order it online from Anchor. Alternatively, melt butter and add some Louisiana hot sauce. It's not quite the same, but it works.

CHINESE-HAWAIIAN BARBECUED RIBS

1950, DON THE BEACHCOMBER, WAIKIKI BEACH, HAWAII

Donn Beach was born Ernest Raymond Beaumont Gantt in Texas in 1907, but had a court change his name after his restaurant's success. He was a prewar visitor to the South Pacific and Honolulu and fell in love with it. In 1933, after Prohibition was repealed, Donn established the first South Sea Island restaurant in Hollywood, where he offered exotic rum cocktails and South Sea feasts.

DON THE BEACHCOMBER, Creator of the internationally famous Zombie, drinks a glass of milk. Zombies—never touch 'em, he says.

In 1947 Donn signed a three-quarter-acre sublease from the Matson Navigation Co., the lessee of the Queen Emma estate, which ran until 1956. While his Waikiki restaurant and bar were being planned and built, he opened the Aloha Hale on Kalakua Avenue, which offered lunch buffets featuring Cantonese food. In 1956 he opened the new Don the Beachcomber restaurant, which offered a Canton dinner, a Moon Festival that featured ribs, a Shanghai dinner, and a Rice Harvest dinner, and also specialized in charcoal-broiled dinners like steak, mahi-mahi, and lobster. In 1961 Donn grew "tired of the old," as he told one newspaper reporter, and sold his business to Mrs. Kinau Wilder, who intended to rename it to Duke Kahanamoku's. These ribs were one of their specialty dishes.

SERVES ABOUT 4

1 inch ginger root, peeled

½ clove garlic

½ cup soy sauce

¾ cup sugar

½ cup ketchup

2 ounces sherry

1 teaspoon salt

1 pound pork ribs

1. Crush the ginger and garlic together and add the remaining ingredients, except the ribs.

2. Place the ribs on a baking rack that's been placed on a baking sheet and rub enough of the mixture to cover the ribs on both sides.

3. Marinate for 3 hours in the refrigerator.

4. Preheat the oven to 325°F and cook for 1 hour. Use the extra marinade to baste the ribs while cooking.

5. Remove the ribs from the oven and allow to sit for about 15 minutes.

6. Slice into individual ribs and serve hot.

ZOMBIE

1934, DON THE BEACHCOMBER, HOLLYWOOD, CALIFORNIA

Donn Beach created this cocktail for a friend who was at the bar of his Hollywood establishment. His friend said, "I'm flying to San Francisco in an hour. Make me something long, tall, and potent." Donn whipped up the now-famous Zombie, which included several rums and fruit juices. He said of his friend at the bar, "He drank two and asked I make him a third to take along with him." After the traveler arrived in San Francisco, he said he "came to" several hours later and found himself sitting on a dock on San Francisco Bay. Before leaving Hollywood, he had a fight with his chauffeur and caused the plane to be delayed. In 1946 Donn recalled the incident: "He wanted to know what I did to him. He said he had a numb feeling—a feeling that he was dead. I said to myself, and I decided to call it the Zombie. . . . No sane person orders more than twice at one sitting, should only be drunk between 4 and 7 p.m. I designed it to be a good conversational drink while playing chess or just chatting. Incidentally, I don't drink them."

Continued . . .

Donn's cocktail recipes were closely guarded and even coded, so no one really knows what's in his Zombie. However, Trader Vic—aka Victor Jules Bergeron Jr., the creator of the Mai Tai—knew Donn well. In his 1946 recipe book, he wrote, "There has been much argument about the origination of the Zombie, but credit should be given where credit is due. Don the Beachcomber, of Hollywood, Chicago, and anywhere in the South Pacific, is the originator of this famous drink. Only he can give you the original recipe, but I can give you my version. Here's my idea of a killer-diller. Why people drink them I don't know, but I'll bet you make one before you throw this book away, and I'll bet you drink more of these than any other drink in the book. Don the Beachcomber originated the drink and since then there have been as many different formulas as there are for Planter's Punch. Here's a simplified version for home use." Vic added, "This drink may also be made in large quantities for use in punch bowls. Oh-ho, what a party that'll be! Personally, I think it's too damn strong but people seem to like it that way."

MAKES 1 DRINK

1 ounce Jamaican rum (Red Heart or Myers's)

2 ounces Puerto Rican rum (Ron Merito or Brugal)

½ ounce Demerara 151 proof (Lemon Hart)

1 ounce orange Curaçao (DeKuyper or Nuyen)

1 ounce freshly squeezed lemon juice

1 ounce freshly squeezed orange juice

½ ounce grenadine

1 dash Pernod or Herbsaint

Put the ingredients in a large mixing glass with a big piece of ice. Stir well and pour over cracked ice in a 14-ounce chimney glass.

SAUERKRAUT BALLS

1803, GOLDEN LAMB, LEBANON, OHIO

The Golden Lamb began offering food and shelter to road-weary customers in 1803, which is the same year Ohio became a state. Since its beginnings it has been a gathering place for the community as well as travelers. Its history begins with Jonas Seaman, who paid four dollars on December 23, 1803, to operate "a house of Public Entertainment." The building was a two-story log cabin on lot No. 58 in the town of Lebanon. It was around this time that the tavern was first called the Golden Lamb. Many early pioneers could not read, so giving a tavern a name that could easily be drawn and recognized, like Black Horse or Golden Lamb, made a lot of sense.

The tavern changed hands frequently until 1843, when Calvin Bradley sold it to Isaac Stubbs. In 1845 it became known as the Lebanon House and stayed in the Stubbs family until 1914. In 1926 longtime owner Robert "Bob" Jones leased the business with C. A. Robertson and the name fluctuated between Lebanon House and Lebanon Hotel. Two years later, Jones and Paul Niswonger bought the building and the business and it became the Golden Lamb once again. The Jones family still owns the building to this day.

As for the origins of this recipe? Well, it started with a woman named Edith who was from Cleveland. She was an accountant who moved to Lebanon when Arthur Portman took over a Clark dealership in 1957. When she came down to help with the books, she stayed at the Golden Lamb. On one of her visits, she shared a family recipe for sauerkraut balls with chef Norm Sims. He was a fried chicken pro and no stranger to deep-fat cooking, and he liked the recipe. So much, in fact, that he added it to the Lamb's menu and it's their signature appetizer to this day.

MAKES SEVERAL DOZEN BALLS

2 pounds pork loin, cut into chops

1 pound ham, diced in ½-inch cubes

1 white onion, sliced

2 pounds sauerkraut, divided

½ pound plus ½ cup flour, divided

2 tablespoons mustard powder

1 tablespoon salt

1 teaspoon white pepper

6 eggs

Panko bread crumbs, for coating

Canola oil, for frying

Cocktail sauce and spicy mustard, for serving

1. In a large skillet over medium heat, sauté the pork chops until cooked through.

2. Remove the chops and add the ham, onions, and 1 pound sauerkraut to the skillet. Cook until the onions are translucent, then stir in ½ pound flour and the mustard powder. Cook, stirring, for 5 minutes or until the flour is absorbed.

3. Cube the pork chops.

4. Combine the contents of the skillet with the salt, white pepper, and cubed chops in a large bowl. Mix well and then let the mixture cool in the fridge for 1 hour.

5. Once cool, chop the mixture in a food processor until relatively uniform, working in batches if necessary. Stir in the remaining 1 pound sauerkraut, then return the mixture to the fridge for at least 1 hour to set.

6. Once set, whisk the eggs with ½ cup water to make an egg wash.

7. Shape the mixture into golf-ball-size spheres and coat each completely in flour, then egg wash, then panko.

8. Deep-fry the balls for several minutes at 375°F. These can be made ahead of time or fried to order.

9. Serve with cocktail sauce and a spicy mustard.

LAMB FRIES

1910, CATTLEMEN'S STEAKHOUSE, OKLAHOMA CITY, OKLAHOMA

The Cattlemen's Cafe opened to feed hungry cowboys, ranchers, cattle haulers, and others in 1910. The Stockyards City area was a beehive of activity back then, as herds of cattle were driven to Oklahoma City in an unending stream to satisfy the East's growing demand for beef. By 1926, Stockyards City was the home of two major meat processors and the area became known as "Packing Town."

It was in 1926 that H. V. "Homer" Paul took over the well-known Cattlemen's. It was one of the few places that stayed open after sundown and it attracted a very colorful clientele. During Prohibition the cafe was known for its home-brewed "liquid delights." In 1929 Henry "Hank" Frey became the owner, and his wife Gertrude was one of his waitresses. He also employed his brother and brother-in-law as waiters. Hank kept the business until Christmas Eve 1945. He was sitting in a smoke-filled room at the old Biltmore Hotel in downtown Oklahoma City, engaged in a craps game with Gene Wade, a local rancher. Frey's luck was running out, so he put Cattlemen's up as the pot if Wade could roll a "hard six," otherwise known as two threes. Wade put up his life savings, which was a sizable amount of money. With one roll of the dice, Frey was out and Gene Wade was in the restaurant business. The "33" brand on the wall of Cattlemen's Hereford Room became a well-known symbol of Wade's good fortune. Wade modified the business name, changing it to Cattleman's Drive-In in the early to mid 1950s, but by 1957 it became Cattleman's Steakhouse and still is today.

Cattlemen's has been famous for their lamb fries for many years. The history of the lamb fries (okay, yes, they are what you think they are—testicles) goes back to when packing houses backed up to the restaurant. There wasn't a market for testicles (who would have guessed?), so the packers would throw them into boxes of meat being delivered to Cattlemen's. Not wanting to waste them, the cooks peeled, sliced, and breaded and fried them and placed them on the plates of steak as a garnish. They became so popular that folks began ordering them separately. Today Cattlemen's purchases 25,000 to 30,000 pounds per year and it's their best-selling appetizer.

SERVES 4

12 ounces lamb testicles, frozen

1 cup cracker meal

Oil, for frying

1. Buy whole lamb testicles from a butcher. To prepare them, they need to be slightly "tempered" from a solid frozen state. They still need to be hard, as they will not slice properly if they are thawed out.

2. Peel the outside membrane away. Using a sharp serrated knife, slice them very thinly, about ⅛ inch. They may be sliced a couple of hours ahead of time and refrigerated or used right away.

3. Roll the slices directly into the cracker meal and make sure all surface areas are covered.

4. Add enough oil to a frying pan to 1 inch deep. Heat to 360°F.

5. Gently drop the breaded slices of lamb testicles into the hot oil and fry for about 4 to 5 minutes. Turn once or twice to evenly brown. Strain them onto paper towels.

6. Serve immediately! They must be served hot. Serve with your favorite cocktail sauce and a squeeze from a fresh lemon wedge.

NEW ENGLAND
CLAM CHOWDER

1826, UNION OYSTER HOUSE, BOSTON, MASSACHUSETTS

The Union Oyster House was opened by the Atwood family in October 1826, when it was simply called Atwood's. In 1853 a pair by the name of William and Hawes were the owners, and by 1855 Hawes became the sole proprietor. In the 1860s Hawes took on Allen H. Bacon as a partner and it became Atwood & Bacon's and stayed that way well into the early 1900s, even after Hawes died in 1897. These gentlemen offered a variety of fresh seafood and their menu also included toast, crackers, eggs, bread, and pies, along with tea, coffee, milk, ginger ale, and sarsaparilla.

By the time the establishment was celebrating its hundred-year anniversary, it was being called the Union Oyster House. Their longtime expert oyster shucker was a Donegal, Ireland,

native named James Farren, who was employed by the restaurant in 1869 and worked there for over fifty-five years. Around 1914 the Greaves brothers took it over and it remained in the family until the 1970s, when the current owners took over. While no one really knows who created the creamy clam chowder, the Union is one of America's oldest restaurants and has served their chowder since its opening.

SERVES 8–10

1 quart soft clams

¾ cup diced salt pork or bacon

3 small onions, sliced

4 cups diced potatoes

2 tablespoons flour

2 teaspoons salt

⅛ teaspoon pepper

2½ cups boiling water

1 quart milk, scalded

2 tablespoons butter

1. Shuck the clams and reserve the liquor. Remove the round muscle and discard. Mince the clams and set aside.

2. Fry the pork in a deep soup pot over medium-high heat, then add the onions and fry until golden brown. Remove from the heat and add a layer of potatoes and sprinkle with half of the flour, salt, and pepper.

3. Add the clams, then another layer of potatoes and the remaining flour, salt, and pepper. Add the water and simmer until the potatoes are tender.

4. Combine the milk, clam liquor, and butter and then add to the pot.

5. Simmer for 5 minutes. Serve with crackers.

MANHATTAN CLAM CHOWDER

1938, DUNLEAVY'S RESTAURANT AND COCKTAIL LOUNGE, HAINESPORT, NEW JERSEY

It's interesting that cookbook author and chef James Beard described this chowder as "that rather horrendous soup called Manhattan clam chowder . . . resembles a vegetable soup that accidentally had some clams dumped into it." Despite how Beard felt about the chowder, it became popular in New York in the late 1890s and its popularity spread from there.

Fast-forward to 1938 when Frank Sciapanski built his log cabin restaurant along Rancocas Creek when it was rural country. He named it Frank's Log Cabin Restaurant, and they've been serving their signature clam chowder for as long as anyone can remember. Frank sold the business in 1975 to the Kaminskis, who sold it to the Dunleavys in 1977. In addition to the clam chowder, they've been serving an open-faced hot roast beef or roast

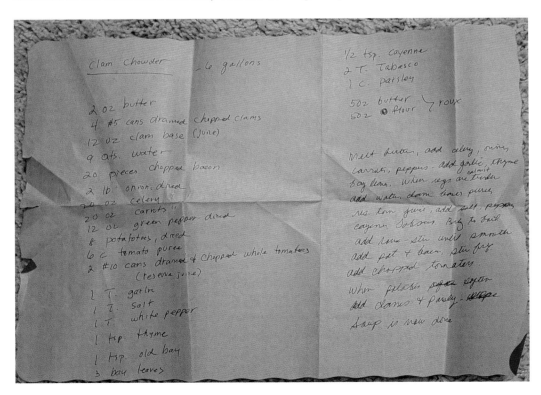

turkey platter with mashed potatoes and "shrimp in the basket" with killer cocktail sauce for decades. When I go back to New Jersey, I always make a stop here, and during a late 1990s visit I asked the chef for the clam chowder recipe. He sent out his copy that made three gallons! I had nothing to write on, so I flipped the tablemat over and used it. This is my conversion of Frank's clam chowder.

SERVES 8

2 teaspoons butter

1½ cups diced celery

1½ cups diced onions

1½ cups diced carrots

¼ cup diced green bell pepper

¼ teaspoon diced garlic

Pinch of thyme

1 bay leaf

3 cups clam broth

½ cup tomato puree

¼ teaspoon salt

Pinch of cayenne pepper

¼ teaspoon white pepper

Pinch of Old Bay Seasoning

½ teaspoon Tabasco sauce

1 tablespoon butter, for roux

1 tablespoon flour, for roux

1 medium potato, peeled and diced

2 slices cooked bacon, chopped

2 cups whole tomatoes, chopped and juice reserved

2 cups clams, drained (liquid used for clam broth)

1½ tablespoons chopped parsley

1. Melt butter in a soup pot over medium heat. Add celery, onions, carrots, and green pepper and cook until soft.

2. Add garlic, thyme, and bay leaf. Sauté for a few minutes to soften garlic.

3. When all the vegetables are soft, add clam broth, tomato puree, and reserved tomato juice. Add salt, cayenne, white pepper, Old Bay, and Tabasco and bring to a boil.

4. For the roux, melt butter in a small saucepan over low heat. Add flour and cook for 2 minutes.

5. Add the roux to the soup pot and stir until smooth. Reduce the heat to medium-high and add potato, bacon, and chopped tomatoes. Continue to cook until the potatoes are soft, stirring frequently.

6. When the potato is cooked, add the clams and parsley. Taste for seasoning and it's ready to eat.

SHE-CRAB SOUP

1763, JOHN RUTLEDGE HOUSE INN, CHARLESTON, SOUTH CAROLINA

The Rutledge House was built by John Rutledge around 1763 and served as a residence for various people until 1853, when Thomas Gadsden bought it and turned it into the Mills House Hotel. After that a number of people owned the building and it often served as a private residence. In 1902 Robert Goodwyn Rhett bought the property and used it as his residence. He soon became the mayor and entertained high-profile guests at this house, including President William Taft.

We know this soup was created in the 1920s by the Rhetts' butler (yes, it's like right out of *Gone With the Wind*), William Deas. No doubt there were other versions of similar soups before he created his, but the roe is what makes his unique. Deas was born on James Island, South Carolina, in the 1890s. He started working for the Rhetts as Goodwyn's butler, but also worked in the kitchen for Mrs. Rhett. He started working for them around 1918 and stayed until Goodwyn's death in 1939 or possibly later.

There are a couple of stories of how the soup was created. One is that Mayor Rhett was expecting a visit from President Taft during his tour of Charleston and he wanted to do something special for him. That's when Rhett asked his butler to "dress up" their typical crab soup. His presidential variation featured orange crab eggs, which gave the soup a bright color and great taste. Another version is that Deas knew how to be frugal when he shopped. Because she-crabs are smaller than the males, they were cheaper, so he decided to use the females with their bright orange eggs in the soup and his creation was born. In 1930 Blanche Rhett introduced a cookbook called *200 Years of Charleston Cooking* and it included

RES. OF EDWᵈ RUTLEDGE,
Broad St. Charleston S.C.

the she-crab soup recipe. *The Index-Journal* of Greenwood, South Carolina, noted in their May 23, 1930, report of the book, "One observes with pleasure that 'William Deas, Mrs. Rhett's able butler, one of the great cooks of the world,' was consulted in the preparation of the recipes."

Deas was indeed an excellent cook and in 1941 became a cook at a popular King Street restaurant, which Everett Presson later bought. One newspaper reported that Deas prepared his signature soup for Presson to welcome him as the new owner. Presson was thrilled with it and made Deas his new head chef and, of course, served his signature soup. In the 1950s when Presson moved Everett's Restaurant to the outskirts of town, he had a special dining room created and named it after Deas, who worked for Presson until he died in 1961.

Regardless of how it was invented, she-crap soup was an instant sensation and has become synonymous with Charleston. The orange-hued eggs, or roe, of she-crabs give the soup extra flavor and color, but this recipe can be modified if you can't get she-crabs with roe. Since they are difficult to find in many parts of the country, white crabmeat can be substituted. Hard-boiled egg yolks may be crumbled in the soup to imitate crab egg.

SERVES 6

1 pound flaked blue crabmeat

¼ cup crab roe or 2 crumbled hard-boiled egg yolks

1 tablespoon butter

1 small onion, finely grated

Pepper to taste

1 teaspoon flour

2 cups milk

½ cup cream

½ teaspoon Worcestershire sauce

1–2 tablespoons sherry

Salt to taste

1. Place the crabmeat and roe or egg yolks into a double boiler with the water simmering beneath it. Add the butter, onion, and pepper to taste and simmer for 5 minutes.

2. Add the flour and blend until smooth. Slowly add the milk and cream, stirring constantly with a whisk. Add the Worcestershire sauce, sherry, and salt to taste.

3. Simmer the soup over low heat for 30 minutes.

PEANUT SOUP

1882, HOTEL ROANOKE, ROANOKE, VIRGINIA

The Hotel Roanoke was built in 1882 in a wheat field on a little hill in a tiny hamlet called Big Lick. Enterprising railroad magnate Frederick J. Kimball chose it as the site of a railroad juncture and a major city. It began as a rambling wooden structure of less than three dozen rooms. As the city grew, the railroad consistently provided resources for additions, remodeling, and furnishings to maintain the hotel's reputation for excellence. After Kimball combined two of his railroads into the Norfolk and Western Railway, he built his vision of a comprehensive community with the Hotel Roanoke as its grand centerpiece. Travelers came to the city or took a break after a tiring rail journey and made the Hotel Roanoke their haven. Over the years the hotel was renovated and expanded to become what it is today.

The Hotel Roanoke has had several chefs over the years and by 1890 had become known for its culinary excellence and elaborate banquets. That year, the hotel hired a Frenchman named F. A. Archambault. He was under thirty years old and had cooked at the Grand Hotel in Paris and London and also at the famous Delmonico's in New York. He prepared delicious French cuisine, which was trendy at the time, but over the years learned to embrace

Virginia's bounty. In 1937 Fred R. Brown became the hotel's chef and by 1940 he began offering Southern specialty items like spoon bread and peanut soup. Brown remained the chef until at least 1960 and he even served Eleanor Roosevelt and General Dwight D. Eisenhower. In fact, his soup became so popular that the recipe appeared in the local newspapers several times over the years. This recipe is the current chef's take on an old Virginia favorite.

SERVES 10

¼ **pound butter**

1 **small onion, diced**

2 **stalks celery, diced**

3 **tablespoons flour**

2 **quarts hot chicken broth**

1 **pint peanut butter**

⅓ **teaspoon celery salt**

1 **tablespoon lemon juice**

½ **cup ground peanuts**

1. Melt butter in a soup pot. Add onion and celery and sauté for 5 minutes, but do not brown.

2. Add flour and mix well. Add hot chicken broth and cook for ½ hour.

3. Remove from stove, strain, and add peanut butter, celery salt, and lemon juice.

4. Sprinkle ground peanuts on soup just before serving.

VICHYSSOISE

1910, RITZ-CARLTON HOTEL, NEW YORK, NEW YORK

This cold soup was invented by a Frenchman named Louis Diat while he was the chef at the Ritz-Carlton on 46th Street and Madison Avenue. His passion for cooking came from watching his mother cook in their humble French kitchen in the 1890s. He was born in Montmarault, France, in 1885 and at the age of eight began to cook and bake with his mother and grandmother. His first dishes were onion soup and potatoes paysanne, but he also learned to bake tarts and broil chickens over charcoal. Diat noted this about cooking: "They are very particular in France."

At fourteen, he was apprenticed to the chef of a pastry shop in Moulins, near Vichy, and at eighteen he worked at various hotels in Paris and then in London. In a twist of fate, William Harris and Robert W. Goelet built the Ritz-Carlton Hotel in New York City in 1910, and it just so happened that Diat was in need of a job in his new country. He started in October of that same year and six years later became a naturalized citizen. His goal was to establish a level of cuisine at the Ritz-Carlton that equaled that of the finest European hotels. He had complete and total support from the hotel's manager, Albert Keller, and Diat spared no expense to meet his goals.

He was accustomed to certain products in France, and when he couldn't find an item that was up to his standards, he asked local farmers to grow it for him. It was the same with the cream in the city, which he didn't like, so he located a Vermont farm with cream comparable to that which was produced in Normandy. Diat also had huge tanks installed in the kitchen to hold trout and lobsters, added a French bakery oven, and imported a Parisian boulangère to run it. Diat's domain covered two floors of the hotel basement so he was able to add an ice cream plant, huge coffee roasters, a patisserie, and a fully equipped candy factory. He also supervised a staff of over a hundred trained employees who held to the highest standards.

In November 1941 gourmets, epicures, and food experts gathered for a celebratory lunch at the Ritz-Carlton to honor the publication of Diat's new book, *Cooking a la Ritz*. They also celebrated his thirty years of service at the hotel and, yes, they served cream vichyssoise glace along with stuffed avocados Ritz, spring chicken bourguignonne, new California peas a l'étuvée, coute aux fruites flambees Jamaica, and demi-tasse. This was all accompanied by Meursault and Charmes Chambertin wine, along with champagne.

In January 1943 Demelria Taylor of the *Los Angeles Times* wrote, "Born in France . . . M. Diat is one of the most famous among the clever chefs of America. He is a tall, slender, courtly man—very handsome with his iron-gray hair, heavy black brows, and dark, luminous eyes.

Kindly, diffident in manner, he is nevertheless an exacting boss over the maze of kitchens, pantries and storerooms and the small army that mans them. He is also an enthusiast for American food."

In December 1950 *New Yorker* writer Geoffrey T. Hellman interviewed Diat, who discussed his famous soup's conception. Diat recalled, "In the summer of 1917, when I had been at the Ritz seven years, I reflected upon the potato-and-leek soup of my childhood, which my mother and grandmother used to make. I recalled how, during the summer, my older brother and I used to cool it off by pouring in cold milk, and how delicious it was. I resolved to make something of the sort for the patrons of the Ritz." Hellman noted, "Diat worked out a soup involving a potato and leek puree strained twice to make it extra smooth, heavy cream, and on the surface, finely chopped chives. He named it crème vichyssoise glace, after Vichy, then famous only as a spa, which is not far from his hometown, Montmarault."

This photo of Louis Diat was featured in the December issue of Look *magazine in 1953.*

Hellman also noted that Diat first served the creation to Charles M. Schwab, who was dining in the Ritz Roof Garden. Schwab ordered the soup the first day it appeared on the menu, and asked for a second helping. Diat put the soup on the menu every evening that summer, but took it off as the weather cooled. The hotel got so many requests, however, that it became a permanent menu staple in 1923. Diat told Hellman, "Mrs. Sara Delano Roosevelt, the president's mother, who had had it here, once called me up at five in the afternoon and asked me to send eight portions to her house. I sent her two quarts and gave her the recipe."

Diat was forced to leave the Ritz-Carlton in 1951 when it closed, but he wrote books and enjoyed life until he passed away in 1957. A fun side note: Louis Diat's younger brother Lucien was a chef who trained Jacques Pépin in Paris when he worked under Lucien at the Hotel Plaza Athénée!

SERVES 8–10

1 tablespoon butter

4 leeks (white part only), finely sliced

½ white onion, sliced thin

5 medium potatoes, peeled and chopped

1 quart water

1 tablespoon salt

2 cups milk

2 cups light cream

1 cup heavy cream

Chopped chives, for garnish

1. Melt the butter in a deep stockpot. Add the leeks and onions and sauté over low heat until soft, but do not let it brown.

2. Add the potatoes, water, and salt and boil until tender, about 30 minutes.

3. Remove from heat. Smash and rub the mixture through a fine sieve or make a purée using an immersion blender.

4. Return the mixture to the pot. Add the milk and light cream and bring to a boil.

5. Allow the mixture to cool and then rub it through a fine sieve or blend again. Chill in the refrigerator.

6. Add the heavy cream and return to the refrigerator to chill completely.

7. Sprinkle with chopped chives before serving.

MELON SOUP

1948, RUBY CHOW'S CHINESE DINNER CLUB, SEATTLE, WASHINGTON

Ruby Gum Seung Mar Chow was born in Seattle in 1920. She attended school until she was forced to drop out of Franklin High School at age sixteen to help support her nine siblings after the death of their father during the Great Depression. A year later, she moved to New York to find work waiting tables, including at a gay bar called the Howdy Club. She returned to Seattle, and she and her husband Ping opened the dinner club in 1948. It was an upscale restaurant at Broadway and Jefferson where celebrities partied, politicians made deals, and business got done (and, for a time, where Bruce Lee waited tables).

It was noted in a recipe book that Ruby's was one of the few Chinese restaurants that indulged the American palate with "artificial Chinese food as chop suey. It's all native food cooked by native Chinese." This soup was one of her authentic Chinese recipes.

SERVES 4–6

1 quart chicken stock

¼ pound raw pork, diced

½ cup sliced water chestnuts

1 pound Chinese melon,* seeded and peeled

Salt to taste

1 egg

1. Place the stock in a 2-quart saucepan and bring to a rapid boil. Add the pork and water chestnuts and cook until the pork is done and no longer pink.

2. Cut the melon into bite-size pieces and add to the pan. Add some salt and cook uncovered for about 10 minutes.

3. Break the egg and gently drop it into the soup and serve immediately.

*Zucchini can be substituted for the melon.

WALDORF SALAD

1893, WALDORF-ASTORIA, NEW YORK, NEW YORK

The original Waldorf Hotel was built at 33rd Street and Fifth Avenue in 1893 by William Waldorf Astor. However, due to a family rivalry, his cousin John Jacob Astor IV built an even taller hotel next door four years later. After agreeing to a truce, the cousins connected their hotels through a 300-foot marble corridor known as Peacock Alley. That's how the hotel got its name—a combination of the two! In 1931 the Waldorf-Astoria reopened in its current Park Avenue location. At that time, it was the largest and tallest hotel in the world.

Now, for the story of the man behind the salad. Oscar Tschirky was fifteen when he left his native Switzerland and arrived in America in 1883. He began working at the Hoffman House in Manhattan and stayed there for four years. He then moved on to be the maître d'hôtel, aka head waiter, at Delmonico's in the city and was there for five years. In 1893 he was asked to do the same job at the Waldorf when it opened. Despite not being a chef, he had a knack for

creating wonderful recipes, including the Waldorf Salad that was created around 1893. Nine years later he was promoted to manager of the hotel and supervised all aspects of the Waldorf-Astoria.

By 1901 Tschirky had become so popular that newspapers from all over America asked him for recipes and menu suggestions for breakfast, lunch, and dinner. A year later he wrote a story that appeared in Washington, DC's *Evening Times* called "Is the American Appetite Jaded?" His lengthy article concluded that no, Americans were not jaded and simply enjoyed delicious food. He noted that in Europe, restaurants had specialties. For example, an English restaurant was renowned for its roasts, a French one for its fish, and so on. He lamented, "But here we have to have all of these at once and on the same table. For instance, I serve at this hotel 1,800 dinners a day—all

of which are a la carte. In other words, there is a surprise in every order for my cooks. You can readily see what a cosmopolitan bill of fare I must have ready." He noted that Americans were great travelers and expected trendy and innovative dishes from their favorite restaurants, saying, "I must so tickle their palates that they will be satisfied with my dishes or they will go where they can be satisfied, and someone else will be chosen to do my work."

Tschirky's salad creation became such a sensation that it began appearing in newspapers across the country. In 1896 a Springfield, Massachusetts, newspaper wrote, "This salad is comprised of equal parts celery and chopped, raw sour apples, dressed with mayonnaise dressing. At the hotel, which gives it its name, the salad is seldom served as a course, being preferred with game and is, in reality, called a game salad." It was suggested as a menu item for women planning their meals, was served at many restaurants, and was even taught in cooking classes. Of course, many offered their own spin on this original recipe.

SERVES 1–2

2 apples, peeled and cored

2–3 celery stalks (enough to make 1 cup chopped)

½ cup sauce mayonnaise

1. Cut the apples and celery into small pieces—about half an inch square.

2. Place the apples and celery in a bowl and toss with sauce mayonnaise.

SAUCE MAYONNAISE
MAKES ABOUT 1½ CUPS

3 egg yolks

½ teaspoon dry mustard

Half pinch of salt

¼ teaspoon paprika

1½ cups olive oil

Beat all of the ingredients except the oil for 3 minutes and then slowly, one drop at a time, add the oil while beating continuously. If it gets too thick, add a small amount of vinegar to thin it out.

CORNHUSKER SALAD

1926, THE CORNHUSKER HOTEL, LINCOLN, NEBRASKA

The Cornhusker Hotel was opened by the Lancaster Hotel Company at 13th and N Streets in July 1926. It cost $1.6 million, offered 300 guest rooms, was ten stories tall, and featured a crest that depicted an ear of corn with the husks turned down. Their motto was "Not the Cheapest, but the Best." The hotel also boasted a coffee shop, a barbershop in the basement, a beauty salon, an "Oriental" store, a laundry, a drugstore, and a billiard parlor. Throughout the winter of 1926 the hotel offered dinner dances early in the week. Guests enjoyed a nine-piece orchestra each night with dinner and a special Sunday concert in the evening. They could choose from seven different dining rooms that included the Colonial/Assembly room; the Georgian/Main; the Lancaster, which was used for breakfast and lunch; Hunters'; and two Chinese dining rooms.

Some of the items in the dining rooms featured the corn-themed shield, including goblets, paper inserts for finger bowls, and matchboxes. A local newspaper observed, "It has been found that a crest or name on things which are removable seems to tempt a certain type of guest to carry the thing away with him as a souvenir." The crest was not fea-

tured on the china or silver. A special daily corn menu featured twenty-five different ways in which to serve corn. Items included corn sauté with green peppers, cream soup, au gratin, corn with okra, Southern-style corn, fritters, pudding, pone, omelets, bread, and Corn-husker corn salad.

Michigan native Walter W. Pelkey became the Corn-husker's first chef to run their modern kitchen. He came to the hotel in 1926 with an impressive background. He was born in 1880 to a baker named Ambrose and held cooking jobs at the Winecoff in Atlanta in 1915, the Adams Hotel in Denver in 1920, and the Acacia in Colorado Springs in 1923. He was also employed at the Ambassador in Los Angeles and the Westbrook in Fort Worth. Pelkey's wife Beatrice was also in the restaurant business and was the manager of the coffee shop in the Lindell Hotel.

Pelkey had a staff of cooks to assist him with soups, entrees, steaks, fish and poultry, roasts and sauces, fried foods, vegetables, and cold meats, along with a butcher and a coffee shop cook. There was also one individual called the "relief man" who would act as the pastry chef once a week to make "real" French pastry, plus a baker for bread and rolls, a woman who made pies, and a head pantry woman with two assistants who made pancakes, waffles, salads, ice cream, and fancy desserts. All of the staff was required to wear white uniforms—the men wore jackets and pants and the women wore dresses. Pelkey told a reporter that he was not going to serve "the ordinary hotel watery mashed potatoes." He promised to make enough mashed potatoes with his electric potato masher to last through the two-hour service. The coffee he served was from Mau's "Milady" and was kept in small urns to ensure it was fresh at all times. The Cornhusker offered two types of salad since its opening—one had corn and this one was considered their "green" salad.

SERVES AS MANY AS YOU LIKE—
CHOOSE YOUR OWN QUANTITIES

Lettuce, your choice

Radishes, sliced

Cucumbers, sliced

Tomatoes, quartered

Green bell peppers, julienned

Celery, julienned

Carrots, julienned

Green onions, julienned

Watercress

Anchovy fillets, for garnish

Capers, for garnish

Hard-boiled eggs, quartered, for garnish

Special Olive Oil Dressing

1. Break the lettuce into pieces and layer it with the rest of the vegetables.

2. Drizzle the dressing over the salad. Serve immediately with garlic bread.

SPECIAL OLIVE OIL DRESSING
MAKES ABOUT 1½ QUARTS

2 garlic cloves

½ teaspoon salt

¼ teaspoon dry mustard

⅛ teaspoon white pepper

¼ cup wine vinegar

¼ cup tarragon vinegar

5 lemons, juiced

¼ cup finely cut chives or green onion tops

Dash of sugar

Dash of Maggi Seasoning

Dash of Worcestershire sauce

4 cups olive oil

1. Crush the garlic cloves with the salt and then add the mustard and white pepper. Add the remaining ingredients, except for the olive oil.

2. Stirring constantly, slowly add the oil to emulsify and blend with the other ingredients.

SHRIMP SALAD A LA LOUIS STRATTA

1918, THE BROADMOOR, COLORADO SPRINGS, COLORADO

The idyllic setting of the Pikes Peak region and Colorado Springs was the location Spencer Penrose chose when he planned the Broadmoor. His goal was to operate the most luxurious hotel in the world, and his destination property included something for everyone—who had money. He created a golf course and offered boating and polo. The hotel's interior decorator, Charles Westing of Philadelphia, emphatically stated in 1917 that "the Broadmoor hotel will be one of the most remarkable in the world." By 1920, Penrose was the envy of hotel men across America.

Penrose wanted nothing but the best, so he hired a young Italian chef named Louis Stratta and ensured his waitstaff was trained to European standards of the day. Stratta believed in food both tasting good and being eye-appealing. He was thirty-two years old when the hotel opened and served as the Broadmoor's head chef and pastry chef for decades. Of flavor, Stratta said, "Cookery in America is all going to the bad, since prohibition has come in. How can one get the flavor, the dash, in the food, when there is no wine or brandy? You want to save American cookery? Get them to vote back the liquor, so then we have delicious food again." Penrose did hoard a cache of liquor during Prohibition, but it seems he didn't let his chef cook with it.

Resort guests chose from multiple magnificent dining rooms that included a banquet hall, two private rooms, the palm court, a children's dining room, a grill for golfers, and an enclosed lake terrace. The grand opening menu included cream of chicken soup, Broadmoor trout au bleu, sauce exquisite, braised sweetbreads with pearls of truffles, boneless royal squab roasted with guava jelly, romaine salad and cherries, soufflé glace, and plain coffee. Today guests can choose epicurean delights from the Penrose Room, Ristorante Del Lago, the Summit, the Golden Bee, the historic La Taverne, the Grille, or the Lake Terrace Dining Room. That's quite a contrast from the hotel's one original main dining room. It wasn't until 1938 that the Tavern was added.

Chef Louis Stratta was born in Evira, Italy, in 1887 and began working in his aunt's cafe by the time he was ten. Fifteen years later he was working in kitchens in Manchester, England. It was there where he was discovered by the management of the Antlers Hotel in Colorado Springs. They imported him to the Pikes Peak area in 1912 and he became their head chef. After a brief stint in Houston, Texas, Spencer Penrose hired Stratta in 1916 as the hotel's executive chef. His first job wasn't feeding wealthy guests in the hotel, however, because it was still being built. Instead, he cooked meals to feed the construction workers. According to the Broadmoor's archives, his staff consisted primarily of French, Italian, and German cooks, but the focus was

on creating classic French meals. Except for a stint at the Brown Palace Hotel from 1932 to 1940, Stratta was the Broadmoor's executive chef until 1976, when he died at the age of eighty-nine.

David Patterson, the Broadmoor's current executive chef, respects and honors the history of food at all the Broadmoor properties. Per the hotel, "Our all-inclusive Wilderness Experience menus were also conceived and executed by David and his team to have a unique take on the history of each location." Patterson is proud to be among the handful of men who were chefs in the Broadmoor's long history. This is Chef Statta's famous signature recipe.

SERVES 1

2 tablespoons diced celery

2 tablespoons diced onion

¼ pound cooked small shrimp

1½ tablespoons French cocktail sauce

1 tablespoon lemon juice

Salt and pepper to taste

2 romaine leaves, washed and trimmed

4 slices hard-boiled egg

4 slices Roma tomato

2 tablespoons diced hearts of palm

1 tablespoon extra-virgin olive oil

1. Bring a pot of water to a boil. Add the celery and blanch for 1 to 2 minutes. Remove from heat and place the celery in ice water. Repeat the same steps with the onion.

2. Mix the shrimp with the cocktail sauce, blanched celery and onion, and lemon juice. Season with salt and pepper.

3. Arrange the romaine leaves on a plate and place the shrimp mixture on them. Garnish with hard-boiled egg, Roma tomatoes, and hearts of palm to the side.

4. Drizzle olive oil over the top and finish with freshly cracked black pepper.

FRENCH COCKTAIL SAUCE
MAKES ABOUT ½ CUP

¼ cup mayonnaise

3½ teaspoons ketchup

⅓ teaspoon cayenne pepper

1 tablespoon brandy

Kosher salt to taste

1 teaspoon lemon juice

1 teaspoon white wine

1 teaspoon Worcestershire sauce

Combine all the ingredients and store in the refrigerator until ready to use.

CRAB LOUIE

1942, AGGIE'S, PORT ANGELES, WASHINGTON

Agnes "Aggie" Andreason had recently arrived in Port Angeles from a North Dakota farm in 1942. She needed to earn a living, so she quickly opened a hot dog stand that seated ten customers. She bought the Doghouse from a couple, and her stepfather signed the papers. Aggie married Jim Willis in 1945 and the business quickly grew into a $2 million restaurant and motel complex by 1974. Their resort-motel was on East First Street and was touted as the perfect vacation spot on the Olympic Peninsula. They were only a short distance to Olympic National Park and offered lodging and meals to tourists. Sadly, Aggie developed cancer in 1974 and turned the management of the hotel over to her brother Harold. In January 1975 her husband Jim was named president-elect of the Restaurant Association of Washington and Aggie passed away that October. Jim kept the business until 1995.

Crab Louie, aka Crab Louis, has a hazy history, as do many historical recipes. Different newspaper accounts offer various versions. According to one Vancouver, British Columbia, story, the recipe was created by the head waiter at Tait's in San Francisco sometime prior to

1915. In 1916 the Fairmont was serving Crab Louis. In 1917 a Louisiana newspaper shared a recipe for the Louis Dressing, which noted, "Recipe obtained in San Francisco used upon the 'Crab Louis': very celebrated." This recipe is almost identical, except the one in the paper called for tarragon vinegar, and was one of Aggie's popular recipes.

MAKES 6 DINNER PORTIONS

1 head lettuce

2 cups mayonnaise

½ cup cocktail sauce

2 tablespoons Worcestershire sauce

½ cup milk

2 tablespoons vinegar

1 cup sweet pickle relish

1 large hard-boiled egg, chopped

1 thick slice of onion, grated

3 pounds Dungeness crabmeat

Optional garnishes: crab legs, tomato wedges, olives, carrot curls, green pepper rings, lemon wedges, and parsley

1. Line 6 chilled bowls with crisp, whole lettuce leaves to form cups.

2. Shred additional lettuce to form a bed of salad and place on top of the leaves in the bowls.

3. Combine the remaining ingredients except the crabmeat and mix thoroughly.

4. Add enough of the dressing to the crabmeat to moisten it. Place the crabmeat on the shredded lettuce.

5. Spoon a little dressing over the salads and garnish as desired. Serve with hot garlic bread.

COBB SALAD

1926, THE BROWN DERBY, LOS ANGELES, CALIFORNIA

The first Brown Derby was on Wilshire Boulevard in Los Angeles and opened in 1926. The second, and most famous, opened in Hollywood on Valentine's Day 1929. Two additional locations opened between 1931 and 1941, including one in Beverly Hills and another on Los Feliz Boulevard, near the popular Greek Theater.

Robert "Bob" Cobb lived in Billings, Montana, where his mother, Mattie, ran three boardinghouses in town. His father, Charles Ackley ("CA"), was a wrangler, the volunteer sheriff, and occasionally a substitute bartender for the family business. Bob's family moved to Los Angeles for his mother's health when he was in his mid-teens around 1915. He worked various odd jobs, but eventually found his best skills in the restaurant business. He, along with his good friends Herbert Somborn and Wilson Mizner and acquaintance Sid Grauman, opened the first Brown Derby in February. Bob's wife, Sally, cowrote a book with family friend and noted expert of the Hollywood era Mark Willems titled *The Brown Derby Restaurant: A Hollywood Legend*. She wrote, "Mizner offhandedly said that if food and service were good, 'people would probably come and eat it out of a hat.'"

Cobb's step-grandson, Bob Walsh, recalled his grandfather and the creation of the salad: "What I can state is that throughout my life, it was clear to me that my grandfather paid attention to detail, valued quality, and was frugal. He learned how to be thrifty from his parents and he developed a waste-not, want-not attitude. To him, it wasn't a suggestion—it was a life-rule. Because his parents operated a number of boardinghouses, Cobb was fully capable of going to the Derby kitchen to assemble any number of tasty and original treats from leftovers. Several of the most popular sandwiches were created that way, as well as a few stews. But, most likely the most popular of all, was his salad that he enjoyed. He made it from anything he could find in the fridge and the Cobb salad was born. This is likely to have occurred in the early 1930s and would not be fine-tuned to the version that eventually was placed as a menu selection circa 1935."

Bob Walsh was Cobb's only grandson, and he worked at the Brown Derby in various roles that started with stocking the back of house, as assistant to the kitchen steward, as a busboy in the adjoining coffee shop, and as a dishwasher. He then advanced to junior steward under the tutelage of the head chef. He prepped various items like hollandaise from scratch for hours at a time "to the point that the odors would penetrate my skin." He also made their famous Pumpernickel Toast. Walsh recalled, "I'd handle the slicer to carefully slice the famous pumpernickel bread superfine for hours. The bread would then be mass prepared on racks upon racks of the slices laid out on the trays. Those slices would be painted

The BROWN DERBY
The Brown Derby
The Original BROWN DERBY RESTAURANT

with melted butter and then grated Parmesan cheese would be applied. The trays were then placed in the oven and brought to a semi-toasted point. The waiters would take the needed number of slices from a tray and place on a smaller tray that was put into what I remember was a salamander to quickly warm and have toast-like, not to brown the cheese. They were placed into a basket with a cloth napkin that was folded over the warm toast and served as guests were seated and then again if they ordered a Cobb or Caesar Salad."

Readers may be surprised when they look at the list of ingredients and the preparation, because today's versions tend to omit some of the original greens and how it's served. This is the original Cobb Salad recipe that has been shared by Bob Walsh. He told me, "The recipe I have shared should produce the closest possible version of an authentic Cobb Salad. In earlier published versions by the Brown Derby, the recipe was mentioned for 4 to 6 servings. Over time, my Derby staff and my family found that attempting the authentic Cobb Salad at home for less than 8 to 10 produced too much waste of ingredients and labor. In turn, anything more than 16 to 20 would likely need professional assistance. So, we found that the the 8 to 10 serving size was an excellent midpoint to suggest for those wishing to bring a taste of classic Hollywood cuisine into their homes to share with family and friends." Bob recommends using a food processor to mince and chop the chicken, greens, bacon, and eggs, but you can chop them by hand if you prefer.

SERVES 8–10

2 whole chicken breasts, boned

1 pound thick bacon

6 hard-boiled eggs, peeled

Roquefort or blue cheese, about 1 cup or to taste

4 medium tomatoes, peeled and seeded

1 head iceberg lettuce, washed, dried, and chopped

1 head romaine lettuce, washed, dried, and chopped

1 bunch watercress, washed, dried, and chopped

1 bunch chicory or parsley, washed, dried, and chopped

¼ cup chopped chives

2–3 ripe avocados

Lemon juice, as needed

Salt and pepper to taste

1–2 cups Cobb's Old-Fashioned French Dressing (see on page 78)

1. Split the chicken breasts into halves so you have four pieces. Place the chicken in a shallow pan or deep skillet and cover with about 1 inch of water. Bring to a simmer over medium heat, maintain the heat at a simmer, and poach the breasts for 10 to 12 minutes, depending on their size.

2. Remove the pan from the heat and allow the chicken to cool to room temperature. When the chicken is cool, remove it from the stock (save for another purpose), remove the skin and bones, and

chop the meat finely. You could also pulse it in a food processor until slightly minced. (This can be done 24 hours in advance.)

3. To prepare the bacon, place it onto racks that fit into baking sheets so the bacon is not lying in the grease. Bake at 350°F until crisp and crunchy, but not burnt. Drain off any grease that might overflow into a metal container and save for another use.

4. When the bacon is done, remove it from the oven and place it on paper towels to drain and cool to room temperature. Drain off any remaining grease, then wipe down the baking sheets and allow to dry.

5. When the bacon is dried and at or near room temperature, place it in a food processor (4 or 5 strips per cycle) and chop it to a small (but not meal-like) texture.

6. After all the bacon is chopped, place a brown paper bag on each baking sheet (requires two or three). Spread the chopped bacon over the paper bags and bake at 250°F, checking about every 5 mins or so. The further draining of grease from the bacon will be dense for the first cycle.

7. Remove the bacon from the bag surface, replace the bags, and repeat the process. It takes two or three times to remove most of the grease.

8. Let the bacon cool. When at room temperature it's ready to be used or can be refrigerated until needed.

9. Roughly chop the eggs and place them in a food processor and pulse until they are fine crumbs and uniform in shape. This can be done ahead of time and refrigerated until ready to use.

10. Place the Roquefort or blue cheese in the freezer for about 15 minutes before assembling the salad. Remove the cheese from the freezer and grate it, using a cheese grater or vegetable grater. Set aside.

11. Cut the tomatoes into small dice-size pieces, drain on a paper towel, and when ready to add to the salad, sprinkle with salt and pepper. This can be done ahead of time and refrigerated until ready to use.

12. The five greens should be washed and spun completely dry, which is key to making this salad. This can be done 4 to 6 hours ahead of time and the greens placed in plastic bags with paper towels to keep them dry.

13. Halve, peel, and dice the avocados and sprinkle with fresh lemon juice. Set aside.

14. To assemble the salad, place all the greens in a bowl and toss, then spread them evenly on the bottom.

15. Arrange the chicken, bacon, egg, tomato, and cheese in strips across the greens. Arrange the avocado around the edge of the salad.

16. Bring the salad to the table with the dressing alongside and toss just before serving. Serve with Cobb's Pumpernickel Toast (recipe follows).

COBB'S OLD-FASHIONED FRENCH DRESSING
SERVES 8-10

1 cup water

1 cup red wine vinegar

1 teaspoon sugar

1 lemon, juiced

1 tablespoon salt

1 tablespoon black pepper

1 tablespoon Worcestershire sauce

1 tablespoon dry English mustard

1 clove garlic, minced

1 cup olive oil

3 cups salad oil

1. Blend together all the ingredients except the oils in a bowl.

2. Using a whisk, combine the oils in a separate bowl and then pour them into the bowl with the other ingredients, using a very fine stream while whisking until well combined.

3. Chill and shake thoroughly before serving.

PUMPERNICKEL TOAST
SERVES 8-10

8–10 slices thinly sliced pumpernickel bread

Butter, melted, as much as you like

Parmesan cheese, as much as you like

1. Preheat the broiler.

2. Place the slices of bread on a baking sheet. Brush with a small amount of butter and sprinkle with Parmesan cheese.

3. Toast for a minute or two until the cheese bubbles and the ends curl. Another option is to bake at 325°F for 10 to 20 minutes until the bread is firm and the cheese is melted.

According to Bob Walsh, "While I remember the traditional presentation used grated Parmesan cheese, I have found that using shredded Parmesan (Parmigiano-Reggiano if you can find it) is very popular and well received, and I am guessing my grandfather might have been open to my suggestion if he were with us today."

RUSSIAN DRESSING

1968, MARINA INN, SIOUX CITY, NEBRASKA

The Marina Inn opened in November 1968 and was billed as a convention center for the three states (Nebraska, South Dakota, and Iowa) that converged on the Missouri River in Sioux City. A year later, after many conventions, it merged with the Hilton hotel system. In 1970 the inn offered "distinctive" dining aboard the Swashbuckler, a formal supper club that served steak and lobster. The Paddlewheeler offered casual dining. This is one of their signature salad dressings from 1974. Chef Michael Costello served this dressing on a tossed Boston lettuce salad, garnished with tomato wedges and shredded red cabbage and carrots for color.

MAKES ABOUT 2 CUPS

½ cup sugar

¼ cup vinegar

1 cup oil

2 teaspoons salt

1 small onion, diced

1 teaspoon Worcestershire sauce

1 clove garlic, cut into quarters

1. Combine all the ingredients and refrigerate for a few hours.

2. Remove the garlic, then shake or stir and serve.

GREEN GODDESS DRESSING

1875, PALACE HOTEL, SAN FRANCISCO, CALIFORNIA

William Sharon, who partnered with William Ralston, opened the Palace Hotel in October 1875, which was touted as the largest, costliest, and most luxurious hotel in the world. It cost an outrageous $5 million to complete and featured 755 rooms on seven floors. There were 45 public and utility rooms, and guests enjoyed the 7,000 windows in the majestic hotel that was hailed as the "Grande Dame of the West." Ralston died just two months before his hotel masterpiece opened.

The Palace had a graveled carriage entrance with balconied galleries and white marble columns extending from the marble pavement of the Grand Central Court to the lofty roof made of opaque glass. Hotel guests marveled at the features and furnishings the Palace boasted. Fifteen marble companies supplied 804 fireplace mantels, 900 washbasins, and 40,000 square feet of flooring, which also included rare woods. Ralston needed so much building material that he constructed a brick factory in Oakland and purchased an oak forest in the Sierra Nevada to provide materials for the construction of the hotel. His goal was to make the Palace the most lavish hotel containing the most modern conveniences. It had five redwood-paneled hydraulic elevators, which were reputedly the first in the West; electric call buttons in each room; plumbing and private toilets; shared baths for every two rooms; a telegraph for the staff on each floor; a pneumatic tube system throughout the hotel; and air-conditioning, closets, fireplaces, and bay windows in each room.

In addition, the Palace Hotel had an elaborate state-of-the-art defense against earthquakes and fire, including a cistern and four artesian wells in the sub-basement, a 630,000-gallon reservoir under the Grand Court, and seven roof tanks holding 130,000 gallons of water. Unfortunately, none of this was enough to save the hotel at 5:12 a.m. on April 18, 1906, when a massive earthquake shook the city. The devastation and fires that lasted for three days destroyed a large portion of San Francisco, including the Palace. It took three years of rebuilding under the supervision of New York firm Trowbridge & Livingston before the Palace Hotel would reopen in 1909. It was for this second opening that artist Maxfield Parrish was commissioned to paint the sixteen-foot mural *The Pied Piper of Hamlin* that is displayed to this day in the Pied Piper Bar.

The Palace Hotel's menu read like one from a fine restaurant in a big European city. It included a variety of fish, meats, roasts, soups, salads, vegetables, desserts, cheeses, and wines. Green Goddess Dressing is a signature dish that was created at the Palace in 1923 by Executive Chef Phillip Roemer for a banquet held at the hotel. The event was honoring actor George Arliss, who was the lead in William Archer's hit play *The Green Goddess*. Since the dressing was created, the Green Goddess Salad has become a permanent menu item at the Palace Hotel. In the early years, when there was limited access to fresh produce, the dressing was served with shredded iceberg lettuce, canned vegetables, and a choice of chicken, shrimp, or crab. Over the years the salad has evolved. Today, it is called the Garden Court Signature Crab Salad and features farm-fresh mixed baby greens, locally grown California vegetables, and a generous portion of fresh Dungeness crabmeat.

MAKES 1 GALLON

2 bunches Italian flat-leaf parsley, finely chopped

2 bunches fresh chervil, finely chopped

2 bunches tarragon, finely chopped

5 cups fresh spinach

½ bottle chopped capers

¼ bottle Worcestershire sauce

½ cup chopped garlic

¼ cup chopped shallot

1 tablespoon sugar

6 anchovies

3 cups tarragon vinegar

½ cup Dijon mustard

3 egg yolks

6 cups corn oil

Salt and pepper to taste

1. Place all of the ingredients except the oil in a blender or in a container and use an emulsion blender. Blend on high until smooth, then while blending drizzle the oil into the mixture. Keep drizzling until the oil is gone, then season with salt and pepper to taste.

2. The dressing can be stored in the refrigerator for up to 10 days.

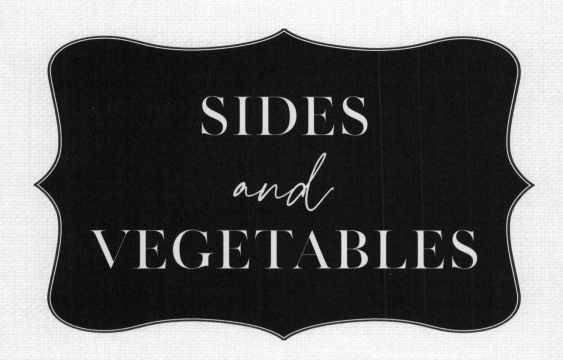

SIDES *and* VEGETABLES

DELMONICO POTATOES

1837, DELMONICO'S, NEW YORK, NEW YORK

This dish is one of many that Delmonico's is credited with creating, likely in the latter part of the 1800s. However, the Delmonico chefs who wrote cookbooks didn't include it in their nineteenth-century books. It did appear in Delmonico's chef Alexander Filippini's 1914 cookbook and as a 1917 menu item under potatoes, as "gratinee, Delmonico." It's interesting to note that in 1878 Louisiana's *Opelousas Courier* and in 1880 the *People and New Hampshire Patriot* published a recipe called Potatoes a la Delmonico, but it wasn't the same as Filippini's. Then in 1886 an English newspaper provided a recipe for them, but it included flour. They also appeared on Boston's Parker House menu in 1890. This is the recipe that appeared in Filippini's cookbook. For more history on Delmonico's, see the Eggs Benedict recipe.

SERVES 2

4 medium white potatoes

¾ cup whole milk

⅓ cup heavy whipping cream

½ teaspoon salt

¼ teaspoon white pepper

¼ teaspoon freshly grated nutmeg

2 tablespoons grated Parmesan cheese, divided

1. Peel and dice the potatoes and boil in salted water until just tender. Do not overcook. Drain and rinse with cold water.

2. In a bowl, mix the milk, cream, salt, pepper, and nutmeg.

3. Preheat a large frying pan over medium heat and add the potatoes and cream mixture.

4. Gently stir mixture so you don't mash the potatoes and cook for 10 minutes, but do not brown. Remove from the stove and gently stir in 1 tablespoon of the cheese.

5. Transfer the potatoes into a pre-buttered baking dish and arrange evenly. Sprinkle the remaining tablespoon of cheese over the top.

6. Bake uncovered in a 425°F oven for 6 minutes or until lightly browned. Serve immediately.

GERMAN POTATO SALAD

1890s, ALPINE INN, HILL CITY, SOUTH DAKOTA

In 1883 the discovery of tin in South Dakota attracted enough English capital to organize the Harney Peak Tin Mining, Milling, and Manufacturing Company. Even though the mill was a short-lived disappointment, the company spent millions of unseen investors' dollars boosting Hill City's economy for nearly ten years and making sure that management lived in the lap of luxury. The company built the Harney Peak Hotel for use by its mining executives. The hotel was a favorite spot for Sunday diners and a rendezvous for mining, timbering, and railroad men active in the area. Even though mining ceased in 1892, the hotel and restaurant survived and remained in operation until 1934.

The hotel was revived in the 1970s by Waldraut (or Wally, pronounced "Volly") Matush, who emigrated from Stuttgart, Germany, in 1961. She moved to Hill City in 1970 and acquired the Harney Peak Hotel in 1974. Over a ten-year period, the hotel housed a variety of businesses until 1984, when it became the current Alpine Inn. This potato salad has been served at the restaurant since Wally opened it and is still served today by the Matush family.

SERVES 8–10

12 gold potatoes

2 ounces red wine vinegar

6 ounces vegetable oil

6 ounces chicken stock

Bacon grease to taste

Black pepper to taste

Chives, fresh or dried, to taste

Bacon bits, optional

1. Boil the potatoes in their skins just until tender.

2. Allow the potatoes to cool enough so they can be peeled and then slice them into thin rounds.

3. Mix the potatoes with the remaining ingredients and enjoy.

FRENCH-FRIED ONIONS

1946, JOHNNIE & KAY'S, DES MOINES, IOWA

Johnnie and Kathleen "Kay" Compiano were a husband-and-wife team who opened a one-room restaurant that accommodated thirty-two people in 1946. They soon expanded and the restaurant and hotel, which were conveniently located across from the airport at 6215 Fleur Drive, were considered one of Iowa's finest at the time. They even became nationally famous when two of their recipes appeared in *Better Homes & Gardens* magazine. They had an open kitchen so their customers could watch their food being cooked over open charcoal flames, and were noted for a fascinating blend of Georgian comfort and contemporary luxury. The Compianos sold the business in 1968 to Hyatt Hotels, which honored their legacy by naming it Johnnie & Kay's Hyatt House. Part of the sale included a provision that prevented the couple from owning a restaurant within a twenty-five-mile radius for five years.

When their time expired, they opened up Mrs. C.'s Kitchen on Merle Hay Road, which later became Poppin Fresh Pies. They were then approached by Pillsbury to join them in a

pilot program for a restaurant chain. They sold their interest in Poppin Fresh and by 1978 started other restaurants, including Gianni's Beef 'N Pasta and the Husker. They were known for their Steak de Burgo, spaghetti, fried chicken, creamy garlic salad dressing, onion rings, and weekend-only red cake with white frosting. They were also known for their three-tiered relish tray with pickled herring and Kay's own creamy Parmesan salad dressing. Newspaper writer Harlan Miller wrote in the *Des Moines Sunday Register*, "I thought longingly more than once of the almost greaseless French-fried onions & potatoes at Johnnie & Kay's or at Edith's, which do 'em better that the Waldorf." Even though Johnnie & Kay's isn't around anymore, you can still have their famous onion rings with this recipe.

SERVES 2–4

2–3 large mild onions (Bermuda or white)

3 eggs

2 cups milk

Flour, for dipping

Oil, for frying

1. Peel and cut the onions into ¼-inch slices.

2. Beat the eggs and milk and pour into a shallow pan or pie plate. Place the flour into another shallow pan.

3. Drop the onions into the egg batter and coat all over, then place them in the flour and coat well.

4. Heat enough oil in a deep pot to float the onions rings. When the oil reaches 450°F, gently start placing the rings in.

5. When crisp and brown on the outside, remove the onion rings to paper towels to drain. Sprinkle with salt and serve.

HONEY CARROTS

1937, SUN VALLEY RESORT, SUN VALLEY, IDAHO

For a detailed history of Sun Valley Resort, see their Hungarian Goulash recipe, which these carrots pair with.

SERVES 1–2

3 carrots, peeled and cut into bite-size pieces

1 cup honey

2 cups white wine

1. Combine all the ingredients in a saucepan and simmer until the carrots are cooked al dente.

2. Strain the liquid out, reserving the carrots.

3. Use in the Hungarian Goulash recipe in the "Main Dishes" section or with another meal.

SHERRIED MUSHROOMS

1937, SUN VALLEY RESORT, SUN VALLEY, IDAHO

For a detailed history of Sun Valley Resort, see their Hungarian Goulash recipe, which these mushrooms pair with.

SERVES 1–2

1 pint whole cremini mushrooms

1 cup cooking sherry

4 tablespoons butter

1. Cut the mushrooms into quarters.

2. Combine the mushrooms, sherry, and butter in a large pot. Simmer until the mushrooms are just soft and have let out some of their moisture.

3. Strain out the liquid, reserving the mushrooms.

4. Use in the Hungarian Goulash recipe in the "Main Dishes" section or with another meal.

SCALLOPED EGGPLANT
1834, J. HUSTON TAVERN, ARROW ROCK, MISSOURI

This area, which later became a small river town, was discovered by Lewis and Clark when they passed by the cliff called Arrow Rock. They camped at the cliff, where they supplied themselves with salt from nearby springs. By 1815 a ferry was established, and in 1829 the town was founded. Five years later, in 1834, Judge Joseph Huston converted his brick home into an inn to care for the many pioneers who trekked west along the Santa Fe Trail. He soon expanded his home, and by 1840 it was widely known as a place where weary travelers rested their heads and filled their hungry bellies. One of the noted features of the tavern was a bell that rang for each meal, emergencies, and special events like weddings. By 1860 the town's population reached 1,000, with hemp and tobacco being the two largest forms of agriculture. The town existed mainly due to the riverboat commerce on the Missouri River, as Arrow Rock's agricultural produce was shipped downriver to the cotton districts of the South.

In 1921 the *Kansas City Star* wrote about Arrow Rock's tavern: "There are two lanterns in iron frames that lighted the doorway when Kit Carson was a visitor. Over the gray brick building, with its vine-clad walls, its old-fashioned flower garden . . . throughout the spacious high-ceilinged rooms with its quant furnishings, hangs an atmosphere and charm that bespeaks the Old Tavern's intimate relation with the past, of times when gay ladies and gentlemen made merry there." This is one of the many recipes served at the J. Huston Tavern over the years.

SERVES 2–4

1 large eggplant

2 tablespoons butter

1 can mushroom soup

½ cup bread crumbs

1 teaspoon sugar

2 tablespoons grated Parmesan cheese

1. Slice the eggplant and soak in salt water for 30 minutes.

2. Drain the eggplant and place it in boiling water and cook until tender. Drain and dry with paper towels.

3. Butter a baking dish and arrange the eggplant in layers, then dot with butter and pour mushroom soup over it. Sprinkle with bread crumbs, sugar, and cheese.

4. Bake uncovered at 350°F for about 30 minutes.

CHEESE BEANS
A LA FALLHALL

1950, FALLHALL GLEN RESORT,
BLACK RIVER FALLS, WISCONSIN

Fallhall was a summer resort in Wisconsin that was situated on the banks of a rushing trout stream on Rural Route 5. James and Maudaline Hall arrived in Black River Falls and opened the resort in 1919. James died in 1936, but Mrs. Hall kept the business going until 1961. Their long-time cook was Lillian Dettinger. It was advertised as being the perfect spot for a peaceful vacation in the outdoors. They served breakfast, lunch, and dinner and were open seasonally from May to November. This is their specialty bean recipe, and the booklet it came from noted, "Most guests at the Glen do not consider their vacation complete without at least one serving of this delicacy."

SERVES 2-4

2 cans cut yellow wax beans

Butter

Brown sugar

½ cup white sauce (see recipe for béchamel on page 33)

½ cup grated cheese, any flavor

½ cup grated aged cheddar cheese

1. Drain some juice from the beans and add enough butter and brown sugar to make the mixture dry.

2. Combine the beans with the white sauce and add the grated cheese. Stir to blend.

3. Place the mixture in a buttered casserole dish and top with the aged cheese.

4. Bake uncovered for about 20 minutes in a 350°F oven.

BAKED BEANS

1920, ROOSEVELT LODGE RESTAURANT, YELLOWSTONE, WYOMING

Indians, fur trappers, and explorers on the Bannock Trail camped in this area where a sage-brush meadow was encircled by Douglas fir and quaking aspen and a mountain stream tumbled toward the Yellowstone River. President Chester Arthur camped here in 1883. In 1906 the Wylie Permanent Camping Company built a tent camp here that became known as "Camp Roosevelt," though Theodore Roosevelt never camped there. The tents were replaced by a lodge and cabins in the 1920s and Lost Creek has shifted course, but people still enjoy staying at this scenic spot on the park's northern range. The lodge, constructed of unpeeled logs and completed in 1920, was originally surrounded by forty-three small log

cabins, the first of which was completed in 1922. Over the years, the Roosevelt Lodge area became a repository for guest cabins brought from areas in the park where they were no longer wanted.

We all know that baked beans have been around since Colonial times, and the lodge's early chuckwagon cookouts likely included beans. When the Roosevelt started having Old West dinner cookouts in the 1970s, they created their own signature bean recipe. It's been a staple ever since, but the beans' popularity really took off in the early 1980s when the Roosevelt Lodge restaurant added barbeque ribs to the menu and served them as a side.

SERVES 8

1 pound ground beef

½ pound bacon, chopped into ½-inch dice

1 medium onion, peeled and chopped into ½-inch dice

1 (16-ounce) can pork and beans

1 (12-ounce) can kidney beans

1 (12-ounce) can lima beans

1 (12-ounce) can butter bean

½ cup brown sugar

½ cup ketchup

2 tablespoons cider vinegar

1 tablespoon prepared mustard

Salt and fresh ground black pepper to taste

1. Preheat the oven to 325°F.

2. Fry the ground beef and bacon together in a large pot, then sauté the onions with the meats. Do not drain.

3. Stir in the canned beans (for thicker beans, drain the liquid from the beans) and remaining ingredients.

4. Place in a large oven-safe bowl and bake for about 45 minutes.

COLESLAW

1947, SKYLIGHT INN, AYDEN, NORTH CAROLINA

In North Carolina barbecue is a food, not a way to cook meat. The Jones family has been making barbecue in the Ayden area for generations. Pete Jones opened his restaurant in the summer of 1947 when he was seventeen. Since that time the Skylight Inn has become a standard in eastern NC barbecue. They have a rich family history and are known for their unwavering dedication to cooking barbecue the old-fashioned way. They started cooking with wood, and that hasn't changed since 1947. The Skylight has been perfecting their vinegar-based BBQ for over fifty years.

According to Sam Jones, the current family owner, "A barbecue sandwich in Ayden is only a barbecue sandwich if there's slaw on it. It's automatic. Our slaw is a simple mayo-based slaw that's sweet and heavy on the dressing. When I say sweet, I mean that we don't even let salt and pepper get in the way. My favorite part of the slaw is the juice that pools on the top of a batch after it's been mixed. I could drink it by the cupful, so I don't like a slaw that's not juicy."

SERVES 8–10

1 head cabbage (about 2½ pounds)

1¼ cups sugar

½ cup mayonnaise

¼ cup salad dressing, such as Miracle Whip

2 teaspoons yellow mustard

1. Quarter the cabbage by cutting down into the core. Turn each quarter on its side and cut down the edge of the solid core to remove and discard it. Peel off the outer leaves and discard as well.

2. Cut the cabbage into 1-inch chunks and, working in batches, fill a food processor to the halfway point. Pulse six times, then run the food processor continuously for 30 to 60 seconds until the cabbage is finely chopped. Stop short of a minced paste.

3. Chopping by hand is also possible, but the texture will be a bit bulkier. To do so, start by cutting each quarter into thin slices against the grain of the cabbage. Stack the slices three or four high and slice thinly again, against the grain of the leaves. You should be left with fine bits of cabbage.

4. Place the chopped cabbage in a bowl large enough to allow some serious mixing.

5. In a separate bowl, mix together the sugar, mayonnaise, salad dressing, and mustard until fully combined. Pour over the chopped cabbage, mix well, cover with plastic wrap, and refrigerate. This slaw is best once it sits for several hours (that's when the precious juice rises to the top), but it's also ready to eat immediately if need be.

6. The slaw is best the day-of because it loses its crispness overnight, but it will keep in the refrigerator for 2 days.

SPAETZLE

1937, SUN VALLEY RESORT, SUN VALLEY, IDAHO

For a detailed history of Sun Valley Resort, see their Hungarian Goulash recipe, which the spaetzle pairs with.

SERVES 2-4

115 grams (a little less than 1 cup) flour, sifted

4 large eggs

Dash of nutmeg

Salt and pepper to taste

1. Mix all the ingredients together until incorporated. Set aside.

2. Boil water in a large pot. Salt the water slightly.

3. Place a large-hole colander over the top of the boiling water. Ladle the mixture into the colander and, using a bench knife or wide spatula, press the mixture through the holes into the boiling water.

4. Let the dumpling noodles cook for up to 1 minute, then strain the spaetzle out of the water and set aside.

5. Use in the Hungarian Goulash recipe in the "Main Dishes" section or with another meal.

RICE MANGALAIS WITH CURRY SAUCE

1904, CLUB CONTINENTAL IN THE JEFFERSON HOTEL, ST. LOUIS, MISSOURI

The Hotel Jefferson opened in time for the 1904 World's Fair, but only for those who could afford to stay there. It was an upscale hotel and was located at what is now the southwest corner of Locust Street and Tucker Boulevard. Its elegant features included marble columns in its lobby, a sculpted ceiling, gilded mirrors, and rosewood furniture.

In 1913 Otto Karl Klopfer became the executive chef at the Jefferson. He was born in Bietigheim, Germany, in 1881 and studied in his own country and Italy. He also cooked when he entered the German army and prepared banquets for 200 officers on the steamship *Deutschland.* When he came to America he worked at the Waldorf-Astoria in New York City and also worked in Chicago, New Orleans, San Francisco, and Kansas City before starting at the Jefferson. In 1935 the Jefferson launched the Continental Club to provide a new hospitality experience. Klopfer worked at the hotel until he died in 1943.

Next came executive chef Camille Mauclair, who was born in Blois, France, and came to America in 1907. He started working at the Belmont Hotel in St. Louis, and after serving in WWI, he spent time in Europe before coming back to cook in Detroit, Atlantic City, Philadelphia, and Pittsburgh. When Mauclair worked in Atlantic City, he served boxing legend Jack Dempsey a crab-stuffed tomato at the Ambassador Hotel. Dempsey liked it so much that his wife contacted Mauclair and he shared his recipe with her. When the Hotel Chase opened in St. Louis in 1923, he worked there and then replaced Klopfer as the Jefferson's executive chef in 1943. The Hilton Hotel company bought the Jefferson in 1950 and in 1955 sold it to the Sheraton company. Mauclair retired in 1956 and passed away four years later.

Around 1950 French chef Jean Raoul Plessis worked at the Jefferson. Plessis was born in Ile de Ree, France, in 1888 and came to America in 1919, where he started as an assistant chef at the Mayfair Hotel in St. Louis. His specialty was curry dishes, like this one.

Chef Camille Mauclair accepting the Order of the Silver Skillet Award in 1953. Chef Mauclair is on the right. On the left is the Chefs de Cuisine Association of St. Louis president Robert Tetart, with association secretary Edwin Keller in the center.

SERVES 10

1 teaspoon oil

2 onions, diced

1 clove garlic, diced

1½ cups rice, uncooked

2 teaspoons curry powder

¼ pound currants

¼ pound almonds, chopped

3½ cups chicken broth

Salt and pepper to taste

Curry sauce

1. Add the oil to a large ovenproof saucepan and sauté the onions and garlic for about 2 minutes over medium heat. Add the rice and cook for about 1 minute more.

2. Stir in the remaining ingredients and bake in a 350°F oven for 18 minutes. Serve with curry sauce.

CURRY SAUCE

SERVES 10

2½ tablespoons curry powder

3 onions, chopped

1 cup diced ham

2 apples, diced

2 tablespoons flour

1½ quarts chicken broth

1. Mix all the ingredients together in a large saucepan and cook over medium heat for 30 minutes.

2. Strain and season to taste.

ESCALLOPED CORN

1904, CLUB CONTINENTAL IN THE JEFFERSON HOTEL, ST. LOUIS, MISSOURI

See the Rice Mangalais with Curry Sauce recipe for the history of the Jefferson Hotel. Chef Otto Klopfer shared many of his classic recipes, like this one, in a St. Louis newspaper.

SERVES 2–4

2 cups corn

½ cup bread crumbs

¼ teaspoon pepper

½ teaspoon salt

½ teaspoon sugar

3 tablespoons butter, melted

½ cup milk

1. Mix all the ingredients together in a bowl and pour into a buttered baking dish.

2. Bake at 350°F for about 25 minutes until golden.

Chef Raoul Plessis demonstrates how to cut filets for one of his recipes in 1955.

RELISH

1922, SAWYER TAVERN, KEENE, NEW HAMPSHIRE

The Sawyer Tavern was built around 1803 and served as a public house from 1806 to 1843. It was built by Abraham Wheeler Jr., a veteran of the American Revolutionary War. His son-in-law Josiah Sawyer later took over the business, and the tavern was known as Wheeler's until his death in 1814. Old tavern account books showed sales and purchases from 1843 forward that included farm produce, grain, vegetables, beef, lamb, and poultry. In 1883 only butter, eggs, chicken, and cream were sold by the spinster daughters of Josiah Sawyer. They owned the tavern until its sale to Lillian Sawyer, who was not related, in 1922.

From 1922 until about 1958, Lillian ran the Sawyer Tavern Tea Room and Gift Shop with her husband Horace, who also had other jobs. Horace died in 1959 at the age of eighty-four, and Lillian passed away at the age of ninety in 1967. The tavern is no longer open, but this is one of their recipes, which they suggested could be used to stuff tomatoes for a salad or as a sandwich filling, or served as a relish.

MAKES ABOUT 2 CUPS

1 tablespoon flour

1 tablespoon sugar

1 egg, beaten

½ cup milk

2 tablespoons vinegar

1 tablespoon butter, melted

1 (8-ounce) package cream cheese

2 hard-boiled eggs, chopped

1 tablespoon chopped onion

1 green bell pepper, seeded and chopped

1 pimento pepper, chopped

Pinch of cayenne pepper

Salt and black pepper to taste

1. Combine the flour and sugar in a large saucepan. Add the egg and mix well, then whisk in the milk.

2. Cook over medium heat until thickened, about 5 to 7 minutes. Take off the heat and stir in the vinegar and butter.

3. Place the cream cheese in a mixing bowl and pour the hot mixture over it. Add the eggs, onion, bell pepper, pimento, cayenne, and salt and black pepper to taste.

4. The relish can be used immediately or stored in the refrigerator for up to about 4 days.

SANDWICHES

NEW JERSEY SLOPPY JOE

1927, TOWN HALL DELICATESSEN,
SOUTH ORANGE, NEW JERSEY

In North Jersey, a Sloppy Joe is not the dripping red meat sandwich that comes to mind when you think of this sandwich. This Sloppy Joe was created in the 1930s from the recollections of Maplewood's Mayor Sweeney, who sampled it at the famed Prohibition hangout Sloppy Joe's in Havana, Cuba. When he got back, he asked his friend and owner of the Town Hall Delicatessen to re-create the sandwich he fell in love with. That's when Fred Joost duplicated the recipe, and the mayor served them at his weekly card game. The original sandwich consisted of coleslaw, ham, cow tongue, and Swiss cheese, with lots of Russian dressing, served on thin rye bread. The deli still serves that, but they also offer this modern version where roast beef replaces the tongue.

3 lengthwise slices of a Pullman rye bread loaf (about 9 x 4 inches), sliced thin to ¼ inch

⅓ pound sliced turkey breast

Town Hall Deli Coleslaw, as much as you like

Russian dressing,* as much as you like

2 slices Swiss cheese

⅓ pound sliced roast beef

Butter, room temperature

1. To make the sandwich, place one slice of rye down and top with turkey, coleslaw, Russian dressing, Swiss cheese, another slice of rye bread, roast beef, coleslaw, Russian dressing, and Swiss cheese.

2. Butter the last slice of bread and place the buttered side down on top of the sandwich.

3. Cut into 8 equal squares.

*There is a Russian dressing recipe in the "Appetizers, Soups, and Salads" section. (The Town Hall's is a secret.)

TOWN HALL DELI COLESLAW
SERVES 8–10

1 cup vinegar

1 cup water

1 cup sugar

½ cup salt

1 head cabbage, shredded

1 carrot, shredded

1. Combine the vinegar, water, sugar, and salt and mix well.

2. Place the cabbage and carrot in a non-reactive bowl and add the liquid brine. Allow to sit for 3 days to brine.

3. Drain well and serve.

CHEESESTEAK

1930, PAT'S KING OF STEAKS, PHILADELPHIA, PENNSYLVANIA

Pat's King of Steaks was founded by Pat Olivieri in 1930. Pat had a modest hot dog stand at the base of the famous Italian Market in South Philadelphia. One day he decided to have something different for lunch, so he grilled some thin rib-eye from the butcher shop. After he grilled the meat on his hot dog grill, he put it on an Italian roll and dressed it with some onions. Just as he went to take a bite, a cab driver who ate a hot dog every day asked what he had there. Pat said that it was his lunch. The cabbie insisted that Pat make him one. "Hey, forget 'bout those hot dogs, you should sell these," he said, and the steak sandwich was born. As the years passed, both employees and customers alike demanded change, and cheese was added. That was the original Pat's Philly steak sandwich.

Since then, the cheesesteak sandwich has become synonymous with Philadelphia. Nearly ninety years later, Pat's is still owned and operated by the Olivieri family in South Philly. As for the cheese? Provolone was the original cheese, and it wasn't until 1956 that they started offering Cheez Whiz.

MAKES 4 SANDWICHES

6 tablespoons soybean oil, divided

1 large white onion, peeled and sliced

24 ounces thinly sliced rib-eye steak

Cheese (American, provolone, or Cheez Whiz)

4 crusty Italian rolls

Toppings of your choice, which could include lettuce, tomatoes, mushrooms, etc.

1. Heat an iron skillet or a nonstick pan over medium heat. Add 3 tablespoons of oil to the pan and sauté the onions to desired doneness.

2. Remove the onions and add the remaining oil. Sauté the meat slices quickly on both sides for about 45 to 60 seconds or until desired tenderness is reached.

3. Place 8 ounces of the meat into each roll, add onions, and then add the cheese. If using Cheez Whiz, melt it in a double boiler or in the microwave and then add. Garnish with toppings.

Do not chop the meat. "It's taboo at Pat's!"

GREEN CHILE PHILLY

1971, CHUTE ROOSTER, HILL CITY, SOUTH DAKOTA

This property dates back to 1896, when it was a lodge for the Harney Peak Tin Mining Company, and was later converted to a barn after the last of Hill City's mining days. In late 1971, Kathleen Elizabeth "Bette" Matkins and her son Marvin purchased the building and transformed it into Chute Rooster. The cocktail lounge opened first and the restaurant followed in January 1972. The business was dedicated to cowboys—both past and present. The name was taken from cowboy vernacular, with a "chute rooster" being a rodeo wiseguy who "roosts" on the chutes and tells everyone how to handle the animals.

Chute Rooster offered a special all-you-can-eat chuckwagon dinner on Sundays and during summer nights. When they opened, they advertised, "Family dining room and hay-loft for dancing. The ONLY Museum with supper club facilities." Their first Easter dinner included glazed ham balls, roast turkey with two dressings, yam balls, "corn puddin'," and Martha's cabbage au gratin, aka gringo cabbage. In 1981 Bette left the business and four years later became the mayor. The current owners keep Bette's dream alive while offering a modern spin on the food served. Prime rib has been a staple on menus across the West, and this is one of the ways they serve it today.

MAKES 1 SANDWICH

¼ **cup sliced onions**

½ **cup chopped red and green bell peppers**

2 ounces green chiles, roasted, peeled, and chopped

7 ounces prime rib meat

2 ounces queso cheese

Brioche hoagie bun

1. Using a griddle or frying pan, cook the onions and peppers over medium heat until tender. Add the green chiles.

2. Increase the heat to medium-high and add the meat. Cook just until no longer pink.

3. Place the mixture on the bun and top with the cheese.

CONEY ISLAND HOT DOG

1917, AMERICAN CONEY ISLAND, DETROIT, MICHIGAN

The American Coney Island was founded in 1917 by Constantine "Gust" Keros, who emigrated from Greece to Detroit in 1906. He was sixteen years old when he came to America and landed at Ellis Island. He was mesmerized when he saw Coney Island for the first time. He loved the lights and the smells of the food wafting from all the eateries, but especially those from Feltman's hot dog emporium.

Gust made his way to Detroit, where he worked at the automobile and pickling plants. He finally settled on a job doing repairs and shining shoes at a small storefront at 114 West Lafayette. He wanted to earn some extra cash, so he set up a little grill in the corner where he roasted and sold hot dogs. Once he started adding his signature Greek-style chili sauce, the dogs were a success. He fondly remembered his days at Coney Island and decided to christen his new creation the Coney Island Hot Dog.

The reason American Coney Island hot dogs are still popular is because they use high-quality, specially seasoned, natural skin casing hot dogs from Dearborn Sausage and their own Keros family secret Coney Island Chili Sauce recipe. Coney Island hot dogs are topped with mustard and sweet chopped onions and served in a warm steamed bun. No ketchup! Gust's granddaughter and current owner, Grace Keros, says, "Coney Island in Detroit is a food—not a place."

CLUB HOUSE
TURKEY SANDWICH

1891, HUBER'S, PORTLAND, OREGON

Huber's has been serving this sandwich since its early days. The business began as the Bureau Saloon in 1879 at the corner of First and Morrison in downtown Portland, but when Frank Huber bought it, he changed the name to Huber's. In 1891 Huber hired Jim Louie, a Chinese immigrant, to do the cooking. In those days, if you bought a drink, you would get a free turkey sandwich and some coleslaw. With just a few booths and bench seats in the old bar, most of the patrons would go around and converse with a drink in one hand and a turkey sandwich in the other. This is how the turkey tradition started at Huber's. They moved to

their current location inside the Historic Oregon Pioneer Building in 1910. Over a hundred years later, they're still known for their turkey.

MAKES 1 SANDWICH

3 slices white bread, toasted

Mayonnaise as needed

4 ounces sliced white meat turkey

2 green-leaf lettuce leaves

1 slice tomato

2 slices bacon

1. Spread the mayonnaise on each piece of bread.

2. On the first slice of bread, place the white meat turkey and a piece of lettuce. Cover with the second slice of bread.

3. On the second slice of bread, place the lettuce, tomato, and bacon. Cover with the third slice of bread. Cut into quarters.

HAMBURGER

1895, LOUIS' LUNCH, NEW HAVEN, CONNECTICUT

According to Louis' Lunch, "There's a lot of debate as to who invented the hamburger as we know it today, but that debate kind of ends at Louis' Lunch, mainly because it's tired of arguing about it, but also because the Library of Congress declared it so. The tiny joint still uses its original cast-iron grills, which cook the hand-ground patties vertically by blasting them with fire. Want ketchup and mustard? Head to one of the other places that claim to have invented the burger: at Louis', your options are cheese, tomato, and onion on toast. That's the way it's been since it 'invented' the burger back in the day, and that's how it'll always be."

THE JUCY LUCY
1954, MATT'S BAR, MINNEAPOLIS, MINNESOTA

Matt's Bar & Grill began in 1954 as a neighborhood burger eatery when Matt Bristol took over a local bar. Shortly after they opened, he explained how the "Jucy Lucy" was created. One of his local customers grew tired of the same old cheeseburger so he asked Matt to stick a slice of cheese between two hamburger patties. Matt did so and presented his customer with the new creation. Upon biting into the molten hot burger, he exclaimed, "That's one juicy Lucy!" No one really knows why the customer called the burger Lucy, but it's legendary now.

There are two stories as to why the *i* is missing from the name. One is that when the menus were printed up, they arrived incorrectly and Matt decided not to correct it. The other has to do with a T-shirt that was printed that included the *i* but it didn't look right, so they took it off.

MAKES 1 BURGER

½ **pound finely ground 80/20 beef**

1 slice yellow American cheese

Salt and pepper to taste

Oil, for frying

Sautéed onions and dill pickles, for topping

1. Divide the beef into two patties and make as thin as possible, almost like a pâté, so the cheese stays in.

2. Place the slice of cheese between the patties and crimp the edges to seal it in.

3. Add a little oil to a frying pan. Once the oil shimmers, place the patty in it and sprinkle with salt and pepper.

4. Fry the patty over medium-high heat for 7 to 8 minutes on one side and then flip the burger and cook for an additional 7 to 8 minutes.

5. Top with sautéed onions and pickles.

HOT BROWN

1923, THE BROWN HOTEL, LOUISVILLE, KENTUCKY

The Brown Hotel was built by a wealthy Louisville businessman named J. Graham Brown. The $4 million hotel opened on October 25, 1923, at the corner of Fourth and Broadway. That night, people jammed the streets for the official public opening. A capacity crowd of 1,200 guests invited to the first of two evenings of celebration could scarcely push their way through the spectators to the inaugural dinner dance inside the hotel. Contributing to the evening's festivities was a ceremony on the street corner.

During the opening week, Brown held the hotel's first dinner party to honor the workers who had constructed the hotel in less than a year's time. He invited 400 guests that included hotel managers, businessmen and government officials from Louisville and elsewhere, and his close friends to formally dedicate the building with a tour, dinner in the Crystal Ballroom, and speeches. Judge Robert Worth Bingham, acting as toastmaster, said of Brown, "Success is never an accident, but comes from courage, character, judgment, and hard work." The public celebration began the next night and continued into the weekend.

The hotel grew and survived Prohibition, the Depression, and the 1937 flood, when the waters of the Ohio River rose over their banks and invaded Louisville's buildings, including the Brown Hotel. One employee recalled, "Food was only served in the English Grill during the flood, but they served three meals a day, cooking with charcoal after the gas and electricity went off. Employees stayed at the hotel and were housed in the Crystal Ballroom, dormitory-style.

According to a former hotel manager named Rudy Suck, "The Hot Brown was developed three or four years after the hotel opened when the supper dance business was falling off. The band would play from 10 until 1 and when they took a break around midnight people would order food. It was ham and eggs, ham and eggs, so we decided we needed something new. The chef, Fred K. Schmidt, said, 'I have an idea for an open-faced turkey sandwich with Mornay sauce over it." At that time turkeys were only used at Thanksgiving and Christmas, and they had just started selling them year-round. I said, 'That sounds a little flat,' and the chef said, 'I'm going to put it under the broiler.' The maître d' said, 'It should have a little color, too.' So, Schmidt said, 'We'll put two strips of bacon on top of it.' I said, 'How about some pimiento.' And that's how the Hot Brown came to be."

MAKES 2 SANDWICHES

2 ounces butter

2 ounces all-purpose flour

8 ounces heavy cream

8 ounces whole milk

½ cup Pecorino Romano cheese, plus 1 tablespoon for garnish

Pinch of ground nutmeg

Salt and pepper to taste

4 slices Texas toast, crust trimmed

14 ounces roasted turkey breast, sliced thick

2 Roma tomatoes, sliced in half

4 slices crispy bacon

Paprika and parsley, for garnish

1. In a 2-quart saucepan, melt butter and slowly whisk in flour until combined and forms a thick paste (roux). Continue to cook the roux for 2 minutes over medium-low heat, stirring frequently. Whisk cream and milk into the roux and cook over medium heat until the cream begins to simmer, about 2 to 3 minutes.

2. Remove sauce from heat and slowly whisk in ½ cup Pecorino Romano cheese until the Mornay sauce is smooth. Add nutmeg and salt and pepper to taste.

3. For each Hot Brown, place two slices of Texas toast with the crusts cut off in an oven-safe dish—one slice is cut in half corner to corner to make two triangles, and the other slice is left in a square shape. Cover the latter with 7 ounces of turkey.

4. Take two Roma tomato halves and two toast points and set them alongside the base of the turkey and toast.

5. Pour half of the Mornay sauce to completely cover the dish. Sprinkle with additional Pecorino Romano cheese.

6. Place the entire dish under a broiler until cheese begins to brown and bubble. Remove from broiler, cross two pieces of crispy bacon on top, sprinkle with paprika and parsley, and serve immediately.

MINT JULEP

1847, WILLARD HOTEL, WASHINGTON, DC

The building that housed the original Willard Hotel was constructed in 1818 and operated as a hotel under various names. In 1847 Benjamin Ogle Tayloe hired Henry Willard to manage the City Hotel, as it was known at the time. In 1850 the hotel was remodeled and the facade changed as well as the name, and it became Willard's City Hotel. In 1901 the old City Hotel was torn down and the current Beaux-Arts building was erected.

The Round Robin Bar opened in 1847 and according to the Willard, "For over 150 years, the Willard has been a major force in the social and political life of Washington, D.C. and its Round Robin Bar continues its legacy as a gathering place for those who comprise the very essence of the nation's capital, guests from across America and around the world. During the 1850s when the Round Robin Bar was called the 'Gentlemen's Parlor,' famous Kentucky Senator and Congressman Henry Clay mixed Washington's first Mint Julep here. The refreshing, hand-crushed libation is now the signature drink of the Round Robin."

MAKES 1 DRINK

1 teaspoon sugar

4–6 mint leaves or more if you like it extra minty

2 ounces chilled Marker's Mark bourbon

2 ounces San Pellegrino sparkling water

1 cup crushed ice

Mint spring, lemon peel, and sugar, for garnish

1. Add the sugar, mint leaves, 1 ounce bourbon, and 1 ounce sparkling water to the julep cup. Muddle the mixture with the back of a wooden muddler (or spoon) for about 1 minute until it forms a tea.

2. Add ½ cup crushed ice and muddle some more. Add the rest of the ice, keeping it tightly packed.

3. Pour the rest of the bourbon and sparkling water into the cup.

4. Garnish with a sprig of mint and top with a lemon peel and a dusting of sugar.

PO'BOY (POOR BOY) SANDWICH

1929, PARKWAY BAKERY & TAVERN, NEW ORLEANS, LOUISIANA

The Parkway's history began when a German baker named Charles Goering opened the bakery. In 1922 Henry Timothy purchased the bakery and continued the tradition of selling baked goods to the neighborhood.

The original Poor Boy sandwich was created by Bennie and Clovis Martin in 1929 at their Martin Brothers' Coffee Stand and Restaurant in New Orleans. In July of that year the street-car operators went on strike. Being former conductors themselves, the Martin brothers wanted to help the men without pay. They put out a notice that read, "We are with you heart and soul, at any time you are around the French Market, don't forget to drop in at Martin's Coffee Stand & Restaurant . . . our meal is free to any members of Division 194. We are with you till h--l freezes, and when it does, we will furnish blankets to keep you warm."

Since they owned a French bakery, the Martins decided to create a large sandwich for the strikers. Traditional French bread has narrowed ends, so the brothers worked with baker John Gendusa to create a forty-inch loaf of bread that was rectangular shaped from end to end, which they called the "poor boy loaf." This innovation allowed for half-loaf sandwiches twenty inches in length as well as a fifteen-inch standard and smaller ones. Early loaves were filled with fried potatoes topped with beef gravy or beef topped with gravy, but other meats or seafood topped with lettuce, tomato, mayonnaise, and/or coleslaw quickly showed up. An oyster shop called Joe's Place in Crowley offered oysters in many styles as well as sandwiches. It's interesting to note that Joe's Place offered a signature sandwich called the Little Giant, which was made by toasting, buttering, and hollowing out a small loaf of bread that was filled with oysters, pickles, lettuce, tomato slices, and other trimmings.

Now, how did the famous sandwich get its name? According to Bennie Martin, whenever he or his brother saw a hungry striker headed their way, one of them would say, "Here comes another poor boy," and would start to make a sandwich. Now, if you're from New Orleans or have ever been there, you know many words are not pronounced the way they're written. So, New Orleans is pronounced "N'awlins" and poor boy is "po'boy." By the early 1930s, both "poor boy" and "po'boy" were being used.

The Parkway Bakery & Tavern, like other eateries, saw the popularity of the Martin brothers' po'boy loafs and started offering their own. Their original sandwich consisted of fried potatoes and a drizzle of roast beef gravy. This is their recipe for a traditional po'boy sandwich.

Vegetable oil, for frying

12 ounces Louisiana oysters

2 cups seasoned corn flour*

1 (12-inch) loaf New Orleans French bread

3 ounces Blue Plate mayonnaise

4 ounces shredded lettuce

3 slices tomato

5 slices dill pickle

Louisiana hot sauce, optional

1. Place enough oil in a large frying pan to fill it halfway up and heat it to 350°F.

2. Dredge the oysters in the seasoned flour and gently place in the oil. Fry for about 2½ minutes or until the oysters are floating in the oil and golden brown in color.

3. Slice the French loaf down the center and place it in a 350°F oven for about 1 ½ minutes just to get a light toast.

4. Spread mayo on both sides of the bread. Place the fried oysters, lettuce, tomato, and pickle on the loaf. You are welcome to add Louisiana hot sauce to taste.

5. Close the sandwich and cut through in the center on a bias. Enjoy!

Make your own seasoned corn flour by adding garlic powder, salt, pepper, and cayenne pepper to the flour to your liking. Store-bought is also fine.

MAIN DISHES

PHEASANT
1940s, CHEF LOUIE'S STEAK HOUSE, MITCHELL, SOUTH DAKOTA

Louie C. and Marguerite Russell first opened Marguerite's Café in the 1930s and then opened Chef Louie's around 1948, where they served a variety of steaks and other items. They prided themselves on only offering the freshest and best meals in Mitchell. In 1958 Louie became president of the South Dakota Better Restaurant Association. When he died in 1965 Marguerite kept the business going for a while and then sold it. They may be closed now, but you can still enjoy this recipe.

Chef Louie Russell giving mealtime grace cards to the VFW on March 6, 1955. Mrs. Eberhard and Merton Tice were with the VFW; on the right is Mrs. Tice.

SERVES 4

2 pheasants

Flour, enough for dredging

Salt and pepper to taste

Paprika to taste

¾ cup milk

1 egg

Oil, for frying

Wild rice

Parsley, for garnish

1. Cut each pheasant in half and remove the skin.

2. Combine the flour, salt, pepper, and paprika in a shallow dish or pie plate. Beat the milk and egg in another shallow dish.

3. Dredge the pheasant in the seasoned flour and then in the milk/egg mixture. Dredge back in the flour again.

4. Heat enough oil to cover the pheasant halves to 350°F. Gently drop the pieces into the oil and cook for 8 minutes.

5. Place the pheasant in a roasting pan, cover, and bake at 350°F for 15 minutes.

6. Serve with wild rice and garnish with parsley.

MARYLAND-STYLE FRIED CHICKEN

1928, LORD BALTIMORE HOTEL, BALTIMORE, MARYLAND

While most people associate Old Bay Seasoning, crab cakes, and oysters with Maryland, they also take great pride in their chicken. It was such a staple that hotels and restaurants had their own take on it, and recipes for Maryland chicken appeared in papers across the country.

When the Lord Baltimore Hotel opened in 1928, it was the tallest building in town and the most elegant. It catered to locals and visiting dignitaries alike, and guests chose from the main dining room, the coffee shop, the cafeteria, or the men's grill to order their oysters and Maryland chicken. The main dining room was constructed of highly polished Crotch Island buff-colored granite and Benedict stone, which is an example of Italian Renaissance design. Large windows allowed for sunlight, and diners enjoyed an artistic fountain of a youth holding a fish at one end of the dining room. It was well-lit with crystal chandeliers and delicate shaded lamps as diners enjoyed their meals while listening to an orchestra. For the hotel's opening dinner and for large functions, they used twelve pieces of china for each table setting, which totaled 24,000 pieces, plus 18,000 pieces of cutlery and 4,000 glasses.

The chefs also enjoyed modern conveniences in the kitchen, which contained no wood because it wore out and was hard to clean and polish. The walls were made of brick, and it contained an electric whipping machine that could "whip as much cream in two minutes as a man could do in four hours." The *Baltimore Sun* also noted, "All of this perfection is merely stage setting for that culinary artist, the chef. His vocation has the touch of artistry about it, and shall always have." They also had Ottenheimer Bros. of Baltimore design refrigerators for the hotel that afforded 8,000 cubic feet of storage and an ice cream freezer.

By 1938 the hotel had its own signature Maryland chicken. It was a tradition to serve the chicken with fritters and bacon, but other sides were often used as well. The dish has many variations, and this is the hotel's version that was shared by Chef Beth Dinice. She told me, "This is standard fried chicken covered with a pepper gravy, and was published in Auguste Escoffier's cookbook *Ma Cuisine* in 1934. Although nontraditional, I do like to add a little bit of chopped chive to my sauce for the chicken. This pairs nicely with a Natty Boh [National Bohemian], which is a historic local brew."

SERVES 8

1 teaspoon dry mustard

1 tablespoon garlic powder

1 tablespoon onion powder

2 tablespoons Old Bay Seasoning

2 cups white flour

1 tablespoon cornstarch

4 pounds chicken pieces, whichever you like

Oil, for frying

½ cup chicken broth

½ cup heavy cream

2 tablespoons cornstarch, mixed with a little bit of water to form a paste

Salt and white pepper to taste

Chopped chives, optional

1. Mix the dry mustard, garlic powder, onion powder, Old Bay, flour, and cornstarch together in a bowl.

2. Coat the chicken with the flour mixture and let it rest in the refrigerator for 1 hour.

3. Fill a cast-iron Dutch oven with oil, leaving at least 3 inches of space between the top of the oil and the top of the pot. Heat the oil to 325°F and fry the chicken until done with the lid covering the pot.

4. The best way to determine if your chicken is done is to use a probe thermometer. Simply stick the probe into the thickest part of the chicken and if it reads 165°F or above, remove the chicken from the pot and set aside. If your chicken is getting too dark and it's not fully cooked, take it out of the oil and cook in a 350°F oven until done.

5. When all the chicken is fried, drain the oil, leaving the bits in the bottom of the Dutch oven. Deglaze the pot with the chicken broth and then add the heavy cream and a little bit of the cornstarch mixture to thicken the sauce.

6. Once the sauce is thickened, add salt and white pepper to taste, along with chives if you like. Serve the fried chicken with the sauce poured over the top.

DIAMONDBACK COCKTAIL

1928, LORD BALTIMORE HOTEL, BALTIMORE, MARYLAND

In 1952 the Lord Baltimore Hotel opened the Diamondback Lounge, where they served lunch from noon until 2:00 p.m. each weekday. It was named after the local terrapin turtle and even used a turtle with a top hat as its logo. Ten years later it was operating as a cocktail and dinner lounge and offered nightly twist dancing instructions by Arthur Murray. This drink was created and served in the Diamondback Lounge during the height of cocktails. Their slogan was, "Your favorite drink made to your request." According to Chef Beth Dinice, "The original recipe, as best I can find, calls for a cherry."

MAKES 1 DRINK

1½ ounces rye whiskey, preferably Maryland

¾ ounce applejack

¾ ounce Chartreuse

Green apple slices and a cherry, for garnish

Pour the liquors in a glass and gently stir. Garnish with apple slices and a cherry.

FRIED CHICKEN

1803, GOLDEN LAMB, LEBANON, OHIO

Around 1927 Golden Lamb owner Bob Jones hired chef Norman "Normie" Sims to run the kitchen, where he created delicious home-cooked meals. In 1950 the *Cleveland Plains Dealer* wrote, "The jolly fat chef, Norman Sims, for more than 20 years has been stirring up his famous black bottom pudding and pie, his sour cream dishes, and his wonderful pecan pie." In 1955 the *Plains Dealer* noted, "The power behind the throne is big jovial Norman Sims, cook extraordinary. No one could fix a dish more delicious than his succulent duck, unless it is his turkey, or maybe his soups. My favorite is his fresh mushroom and cream concoction, fit for the tables of Olympians." In 1961 the *Cincinnati Enquirer* referred to Chef Sims as "the gentleman responsible for the excellent roast Long Island duck."

By 1965 Sims was working with chef William Hooks at the Golden Lamb and the inn was claiming it was the "home of the black bottom pie." The inn listed roast duck and baked Virginia ham as their house specialties, but Sims said his favorite dish was the fried chicken, while Hooks was partial to the tenderloin tips and mushrooms. Some of Chef Sims's other dishes included chicken pie, pot roast, strawberry torte, double chocolate cake, and pecan and lime chiffon pies. It seems that Sims left the inn around the same time that his longtime boss, Bob Jones, leased it out in 1969. By 1968 William Hooks took over as chef supervisor, and by 1970 German chef Erwin Pfeil had replaced him. (For more history on the Golden Lamb, see their Sauerkraut Balls recipe.)

Historian John Zimkus tells the story of a certain Kentucky man named Harlan Sanders who once dined at the Golden Lamb. After eating the fried chicken, Sanders asked owner Bob Jones for Chef Sims's recipe. Bob's wife Ginny didn't want to share the recipe, but Bob agreed and asked Sims to talk to the gentleman, whose name was unknown at the time. When the man returned to his home in Corbin, Kentucky, he prepared fried chicken using his newly acquired recipe. He then served it to his friends in the back room of the gas station he owned.

Zimkus wrote, "To be truthful, upon first hearing the tale, I was dubious of its authenticity. However, around 2008, in my capacity as the Historian of the

Golden Lamb's chefs Norman (left) and William Hooks displaying their creations in 1965.

Golden Lamb, I met Martha 'Marty' Jones Landise, Bob Jones' niece. I told her the fried chicken story, which she had never heard before. She did say, though, they started their drive to Florida for their honeymoon. She recalled that before leaving 'Uncle Bob' told them to stop by Corbin, Kentucky, on their way down south. A friend of his had a motel there, and he would treat them well. That friend's name was Harlan Sanders. About seven or eight years later after hearing this story, I was speaking to a group of Ohio county auditors and treasurers. After telling them the tale, one of the gentlemen told me that he had once met Harlan Sanders. He recalled telling 'the Colonel' that he was from Highland County, Ohio. Harlan asked if that was anywhere near Lebanon and said there was a restaurant there that he had visited several times—the Golden Lamb. Finally, in August 2019, I met Harlan Sanders' great-nephew. He said the events in the story lined up, but from what he heard, 'Uncle Harlan' asked everybody who's fried chicken he loved, for their recipe. We'll never know many, if any, of Colonel Sanders' secret '11 herbs and spices' originally came from the Golden Lamb's recipe."

SERVES 4-6

2 tablespoons sugar

2 tablespoons kosher salt

2 cups water

1 chicken (3–4 pounds), cut into 8 pieces

3 cups oil, for frying

4½ teaspoons chicken seasoning

1 tablespoon canola oil

1 cup flour

1. In a mixing bowl, combine the sugar, salt, and water. Mix until dissolved and pour over the chicken until the pieces are fully submerged. Place on the bottom shelf of the refrigerator with a lid for a minimum of 12 hours, but no more than 24.

2. When ready, remove the chicken from the brine and rinse in the sink using a strainer. Pat dry with paper towels and set in a large bowl.

3. Place 3 cups of oil in a straight-sided pot or cast-iron skillet over medium heat and bring to 350°F.

4. Combine your favorite seasoning (the Golden Lamb has been using its secret recipe for over 100 years) with the canola oil and rub over the chicken to coat it.

5. Add 2 tablespoons of flour and mix to start creating the dredge, then add the remaining flour and mix until chicken is evenly coated.

6. Carefully place the dredged chicken into the hot oil, bone side down. Allow to cook about 12 to 15 minutes. You will see browning on the sides of the chicken indicating that it is ready to flip.

7. Carefully flip each piece and cook for an additional 5 minutes.

8. Place a meat thermometer into the thickest part of a breast, close to the bone, and check for a temperature of 165°F. Remove the chicken to rest on a wire rack for 15 minutes before enjoying.

CHICKEN PIE

1930s, OLD HUNDRED, SOUTHBURY, CONNECTICUT

Potpies have been around since Colonial times and were a practical and economical way to feed a lot of people. So, it's not surprising that many restaurants and inns offered them on their bills of fare. Nellie I. Brown ran the Old Hundred inn and in 1939 published a cookbook called *Recipes from Old Hundred: 200 Years of New England Cooking*. Recipes included dishes like Cranberry Muffins, Connecticut Fish Chowder, Veal Stew with Dumplings, Onion Short-cake, Buttermilk Biscuits, Old Hundred Cream Puffs, and Chicken Pie. There is a note in her cookbook that says, "This is an old family recipe that is used for my famous Saturday Night 'Old Fashioned New England Dinner.' It is luscious." She also noted, "Another special is our Old Fashioned Chicken Pie, 'like Mother used to make.'"

SERVES 6–8

1 large chicken

¼ pound salt pork, optional

Salt to taste

2 tablespoons butter

2 tablespoons flour

1½ cups broth

Biscuit dough (see the Baking Powder Biscuits recipe on page 18)

1. Place the chicken and optional salt pork in a large pot and cover it with hot water. Simmer until tender.

2. Taste the broth and add salt as needed. Allow to cool until it can be handled.

3. Remove the chicken and salt pork from the pan and set the broth aside. Remove the skin and bones from the chicken and cut the meat into large pieces. Discard the salt pork.

4. Simmer and reduce the broth by half.

5. Melt the butter in a large saucepan over medium heat. Add the flour and cook until crumbly, about 1 minute.

6. Slowly add the reduced broth, stirring constantly. Cook until it thickens and season to taste.

7. Roll the biscuit dough to 1 ½ inches thick and cut to fit the baking dish. Place on a cookie sheet and bake at 425°F for about 12 minutes or until golden brown.

8. Fill an ovenproof serving dish with the chicken and gravy and keep warm. Place the cooked biscuit top on the chicken and serve.

CHICKEN KAMA'AINA

1944, THE WILLOWS, HONOLULU, HAWAII

The Willows at 901 Hausten Street was the private family home of the Haustens in Honolulu. Mrs. Emma Kaleionamoku Ai McGuire Hausten turned part of the home into a restaurant that opened on July 4, 1944. The dining room had a thatched-roof pavilion overlooking a flowering lagoon and offered dinner every day except Sunday. Lunch was added two years later. Surrounded by an exotic tropical garden, it was dubbed "Hawaii's Original Garden Restaurant."

The Willows was managed by Mrs. Hausten's daughters, Kathleen McGuire Perry, who also acted as the hostess, and Carol Ellerbrake, who was the chef, and her son Grandison "Grandy" Hausten. In 1966 the *Star-Bulletin & Advertiser* wrote, "The Willows became the first Hawaii restaurant to be named in *American Restaurant Magazine*'s Hall of Fame. Today, 22 years after it was founded, it is world famous for its chicken and shrimp curry and for its 'mile high' slices of coconut cream pie."

The Willows was known for its hospitality and good food. Chef Carol said in 1961, "I tell my girls never to put anything out that they won't eat themselves." At that time, she had a staff of fourteen who produced meals for 11,000 to 14,000 diners a month. She also said, "When I came in, it was just to help out temporarily and I'm still here." She took over the kitchen in 1948 and was considered the bottle washer, too. The restaurant is no longer in business, but you can still create this signature recipe and get a taste of history.

SERVES 4

1 chicken (3–4 pounds)

Pineapple chunks

Flour

Coconut milk

Oil, for frying

Giblet gravy

Freshly grated coconut

1. Cut the chicken in half and debone it. Remove the wings and save for another use.

2. Skewer pineapple chunks onto two sticks. Attach the chicken to the skewers so it covers the pineapple on one side.

3. Roll each half in flour and then dip in coconut milk.

4. Place oil in a deep pot and bring to 350°F. Gently place the chicken in the pot and deep-fry until golden. Remove the chicken and place on a baking sheet.

5. Grill or broil the chicken for 8 minutes or until it reaches 165°F.

6. Cover with giblet gravy and freshly grated coconut.

MAI TAI

1944, TRADER VIC'S, OAKLAND, CALIFORNIA

Victor Bergeron was born in 1902 in San Francisco and was the younger of two boys. His mother was a petite French woman from the Pyrenees and his father was a big, tall French Canadian. His mother cared for him and his brother while his father worked as a waiter at the Fairmont Hotel. In 1920 his parents decided he should attend the Healds Business School so he could learn bookkeeping. He knew he didn't want to do that, so he only attended school for nine months. He worked several different jobs over the years, but he said working as a bookkeeper at the Athenian Night Club in Oakland made an impression on him. He wrote, "This became significant because for the first time I was exposed to food that was foreign to me. Well, that lasted a couple of years and during that time I learned a lot about excellent cooking."

Bergeron had more jobs, got married, and had three children. He took a job at his uncle's saloon, across the street from where his first Trader Vic's would be on San Pablo. He wrote, "I had no idea of how to mix a drink. I used to keep a little book in the room behind the bar and every time someone asked me for a mixed drink, I'd duck in the room and look up the ingredients." His uncle was a "weirdie," as he called him, and after Vic couldn't take his lectures anymore, he quit. His aunt gave him $800 and he walked across the street to an empty lot. He wrote, "Old man Jerky owned this lot on the corner and I propositioned him. I asked, 'How much of a building can you build for $500?'" He told the out-of-work carpenter, "I'll pay you enough to live on and I'll pay you good rent if you will build me a little restaurant." His $500 bought him a 22-by-26-foot building with two toilets and plumbing. He opened Hinky Dink's in November 1934 and the place was packed morning, noon, and night.

After a few years of working nonstop, Vic and his wife took a trip to the Caribbean and to study drinks. Their route took them to Havana, Cuba, and New Orleans. It was after that trip that he started to create delicious new cocktails. The next change came when his two friends, Henry Smith and Bruce McCullen, took him back to San Francisco.

Continued . . .

They wanted him to visit the South Seas and Don the Beachcomber establishments, and he even bought some items from Don's. When he got back, he told his wife what he had seen and she agreed to change the name and decor of Hinky's. His wife suggested the name Trader Vic's because he was always trading with someone. They also decided to serve Chinese food. Vic recalled, "There was no fanfare about the opening. Just closed one day as Hinky Dinks selling sandwiches and opened the next day as Trader Vic's selling tropical drinks and Chinese food. Sixty-five or seventy people were served the first night. Inside of six months, people were waiting out in the street to get in."

It was 1949 when Western Hotels executive Edward "Eddie" Carlson convinced Bergeron to open his first franchised location in the Benjamin Franklin Hotel in Seattle. Originally a small bar named the Outrigger, it was expanded into a full restaurant in 1954 and renamed Trader Vic's in 1960. During the tiki culture fad of the 1950s and '60s, as many as twenty-five Trader Vic's restaurants were in operation worldwide. They all featured the popular mix of Polynesian artifacts, unique cocktails, and exotic cuisine. During that time, Vic took the Mai Tai to the Hawaiian Islands to formalize drinks for the Royal Hawaiian,

Continued . . .

Moana, and Surfrider motels. In 1972 he wrote this in his recipe book: "And old Kama'aina can tell you about this drink and of its rapid spread throughout the islands. Now it is estimated that they serve several thousand Mai Tais daily in Honolulu alone; and we sell many more than that daily in our twenty Trader Vic's restaurants throughout the world."

He also wrote, "There has been a lot of conversation over the beginning of the Mai Tai. And I want to get the record straight. I originated the Mai Tai. In 1944, after success with several exotic rum drinks, I felt a new drink was needed. I was at the service bar in my Oakland restaurant. I took down a bottle of seventeen-year-old rum. It was J. Wray Nephew from Jamaica—surpassingly golden in color, medium bodied, but with the rich pungent flavor particular to the Jamaican blends. I took a fresh lime, added some orange curacao from Holland, a dash of rock candy syrup, and a dollop of French orgeat, for its subtle almond flavor. I added a generous amount of shaved ice and shook it vigorously by hand to produce the marriage I was after. Half the lime shell went in the drink for color; I stuck in a branch of fresh mint. I gave the first two of them to Ham and Carrie Guild, friends from Tahiti, who were there that night. Carrie took one sip and said, 'Mai Tai— Roa Aé.' In Tahitian this means 'Out of this world—the Best.' Well, that was that. I named the drink 'Mai Tai.' Anybody who says I didn't create this drink is a dirty stinker."

MAKES 1 DRINK

1 lime

1 ounce dark Jamaican rum or Martinique rum

½ ounce orange curacao

¼ ounce rock candy syrup

¼ ounce orgeat syrup

Fresh mint and fruit stick, for garnish

1. Cut the lime in half and squeeze the juice over shaved ice in a double old-fashioned glass. Save one spent lime shell.

2. Add the remaining ingredients and enough shaved ice to fill the glass. Hand shake.

3. Decorate with the spent lime shell, fresh mint, and a fruit stick.

CHICKEN
A LA CACCIATORE

1950, LOUIGI'S CHARCOAL BROILER & ITALIAN SPECIALTY RESTAURANT, LAS VEGAS, NEVADA

This casual, informal restaurant was opened by Louigi Coniglio and Howard Werner. Louigi was a Los Angeles bookmaker who decided to go to Las Vegas in 1946 with his wife Mildred ("Millie") and go into the gambling business. Instead, he gambled on a restaurant and partnered with Werner. Millie also worked at the restaurant that originally sat between the Sands and Flamingo casinos. According to the *Las Vegas Review-Journal* in 1960, Louigi's was Frank Sinatra's favorite restaurant.

In March 1962 they celebrated serving their one-millionth customer and broke ground on their new building at 3729 Las Vegas Boulevard farther up the strip. The *Review-Journal* wrote, "His sumptuous new quarters more than do justice to the rapidly climbing standards of fine Las Vegas eateries. The new epicurean edifice is spacious, yet very intimate. Seats 200 people and Louigi has widely dedicated many dishes on his menu to prominent local and out-of-town celebs. The food, as always, is magnificent. The hospitality—Louigi has no peer." Their delicious food included fresh fish and roasted meats. They also offered Italian specialties that included home-made gnocchi, fresh tomato omelets a la Louigi, mostaccioli a la Louigi, Louigi's famous Italian charcoal-broiled sausage and peppers, chicken a la cacciatore, steak pizzaiolo, veal scallopine, and baked lasagna.

The restaurant had a grand opening at its new location in January 1963 and the entire staff, including Louigi,

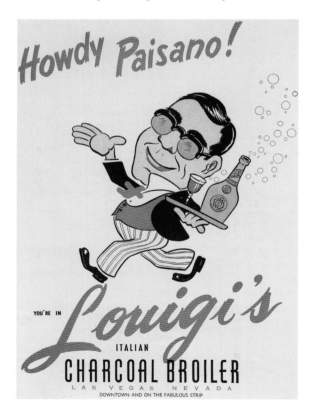

Millie, partner and right-hand man Howard Werner, hostess daughter Lora Ann Compton, head chef and son-in-law James "Jimmy" Slife, and second chef Joe Giglio, were ready. They also had a waitress named Patty Stiefhoff who acted as baker and made all their cakes, pies, and pastries, and mixologists Joe Boulet and Joe Corrigan were at the ready.

Louigi retired in February 1967 when he sold his share of the business to a Dallas, Texas, man named Joe Merrill. He was lured out of retirement for a couple of ventures, but the most prestigious position was when he took over the Gourmet Room in the Tropicana that featured an international menu, and later the Regency Lounge in the Sands casino. Louigi's legacy lives on in his recipe.

SERVES 4–6

¼ **cup olive oil**

1 chicken (about 2 pounds), cut into pieces

Salt and pepper to taste

1 teaspoon minced garlic

1 medium onion, peeled and sliced

2 large green peppers, seeded and sliced

1 pound mushrooms, sliced

1 (32-ounce) can tomatoes or 8 fresh chopped tomatoes

¼ **teaspoon fresh basil**

¼ **teaspoon oregano**

1. Heat the oil in a large stockpot over medium-high heat.

2. Salt and pepper the chicken pieces and add to the pot. Sauté until golden brown, about 25 minutes.

3. Add the remaining ingredients and reduce the heat to low. Simmer for 30 minutes.

4. Adjust seasoning as needed and serve with spaghetti or steamed white rice.

FRIED CHICKEN
CASTAÑEDA
1898, LA CASTAÑEDA, LAS VEGAS, NEW MEXICO

While the Atchison, Topeka & Santa Fe railroad (AT&SF) arrived in Las Vegas, New Mexico, in 1880, it wasn't until 1898 that Fred Harvey entered the restaurant business with this celebrated Harvey House called Castañeda. It sat opposite the train depot and was the site of Theodore Roosevelt's first Rough Rider reunion. The Castañeda was Harvey's first trackside hotel and it covered roughly 30,000 square feet, plus a 500-foot-long arcade. The Santa Fe Railway mainline ran directly in front and connected the town to Chicago and Los Angeles.

The Castañeda was designed by Frederick Roehrig, a prominent Pasadena architect. It was the earliest Harvey House to be built in Mission Revival style, and became the prototype of nearly all future Harvey properties. Harvey's new venture was so successful that in 1902 the AT&SF built the Alvarado Hotel in Albuquerque using the Castañeda's design.

Chef Dan Tachet was known for serving native dishes such as albondigas soup and chicken enchiladas, along with fried chicken topped with tomato sauce served with French peas and squash. This recipe was created by Tachet, who was the chef at this Fred Harvey hotel. It's the precursor to chicken tenders.

7944. THE CASTANEDA, LAS VEGAS, N. M. FRED HARVEY.

COPYRIGHT, 1905, BY FRED HARVEY.

4 tablespoons butter

1 onion, peeled and chopped very fine

¼ cup flour

4 cups chicken broth

1 cup heavy cream

2 egg yolks

3 tablespoons chopped parsley

Bread crumbs

2–3 large eggs, beaten

3 pounds boneless chicken breasts, cut into 1-inch strips

Oil, for frying

1. Melt the butter in a large saucepan over medium heat.

2. Add the onion and cook for about 5 minutes or until translucent. Add the flour and cook while stirring for about 1 minute.

3. Mix in the broth and cream. Stir and let come to a boil. Reduce the heat to low and cook for about 10 minutes.

4. Slowly whisk in the eggs and then add the parsley. Remove from the heat. (This sauce must be quite thick.)

5. Place the bread crumbs in a shallow bowl and do the same with the beaten eggs. Dip the strips of chicken in the sauce so that it adheres to both sides. Lay the strips in the bread crumbs and coat all sides. If still too warm, allow to cool, and then dip them in the beaten egg and then again in the bread crumbs.

6. Add enough oil to a heavy-duty frying pan to fill it a little over halfway. Heat until bubbling gently over medium-high heat.

7. Carefully add the chicken strips and reduce the heat. Cook until lightly browned for about 5 minutes and then turn. Serve with tomato sauce and French peas as garnish.

CHICKEN AND WAFFLES

1929, MILLER'S, RONKS, PENNSYLVANIA

Chicken and waffles in and around Pennsylvania's Amish country is quite different from what usually comes to mind. Southern versions include fried chicken served on waffles with maple syrup. In fact, the dish was served in the nineteenth century at church socials and other fund-raising events. Later restaurants and hotels advertised chicken and waffles as their specialty. In 1907 the *Snyder County Tribune* reported that the ladies of the Reformed church were having a chicken and waffle fund-raising dinner "as has been their custom for a number of years."

Enos R. Miller and his wife Anna lived in Lancaster, where he had a garage and worked on large trucks, but in 1928 he retired and sold his business due to ill health. In 1929 he opened the Rusco Break & Belting Service, where Anna started serving chicken and waffles to the truckers as her husband did repairs. It did not take long for the small, friendly restaurant to dominate the garage business, and that turned into Miller's. In 1948 Beatrice Strauss, a waitress at Miller's, and her husband Thomas bought the restaurant from the Millers. Keeping the Miller's name, the restaurant flourished. In 1954 the Lancaster *Intelligencer Journal* ran an ad for Miller's and it included "Famous for our Chicken & Waffles."

In 1957 the business was changed to Miller's Smorgasbord and they began serving their famous "seven sweets and seven sours." In 1973 Miller's Bakery opened and became an integral part of Miller's Smorgasbord, supplying all of the delicious baked goods and desserts for the buffet. In 1975 Miller's Smorgasbord underwent a major expansion that included upgrading the kitchen facilities and the addition of a second dining room. In 1983 another renovation changed the dining room layout.

SERVES 4–6

1 chicken (about 4 pounds)

5 quarts cold water

3 large carrots, trimmed and unpeeled, for stock

1 large onion, unpeeled, for stock

4 celery stalks, washed, for stock

2 carrots, peeled and chopped into ¼-inch pieces

2 stalks celery, cut into ¼-inch pieces

1 medium onion, peeled and chopped

½ cup reserved chicken fat or butter

¾ cup flour

2 teaspoons parsley

1 tablespoon chives

1 teaspoon white pepper

Waffles (see recipe on page 13)

1. To make the stock, place the chicken, water, carrots, onion, and celery in a large stockpot. Bring to a boil and then reduce heat to a simmer and cook for 3 hours.

2. Remove from the heat and discard the vegetables. Strain the stock into a large bowl and refrigerate.

3. Remove the chicken and when cool enough to handle, remove the meat. Remove the bones, gristle, and fat. Shred or chop the meat coarsely and set aside.

4. Place the chopped carrots, celery, and onion in a saucepan and enough stock to cover. Cover the pan and bring to a boil. Cook until the vegetables are tender. Strain and set aside.

5. Melt ½ cup reserved chicken fat or butter over medium heat in a separate stockpot. Stir in the flour and cook for 1 minute to make a roux. Slowly add 2 quarts of the stock and stir with a whisk while cooking over high heat. Bring to a boil to thicken.

6. Add the shredded chicken, the vegetables, and seasonings. Cover and cook over low heat until everything is heated through.

7. Serve warm over waffles.

GREEN ENCHILADAS

1946, CASA RIO, SAN ANTONIO, TEXAS

Alfred F. Beyer opened Casa Rio in 1946 along San Antonio's famed River Walk. It's housed in a Spanish Colonial–period hacienda with a cedar door, fireplace, and thick rock walls. This is one of their signature dishes.

SERVES ABOUT 10

1 chicken (3–4 pounds)

Onion, chopped, as much as you like

Celery, chopped, as much as you like

Salt and pepper to taste

5 pounds tomatillos

2 green bell peppers, chopped

3 onions, peeled and chopped

3 cubes chicken bouillon

1 pint chicken broth

32 corn tortillas

Oil, for frying

1½ pounds Monterey Jack cheese, grated

1 pint sour cream

1. Place the chicken in a pot and cover with water. Add the onion, celery, and salt and pepper. Simmer over low heat until the chicken is tender.

2. Remove from the heat and strain, reserving the broth. Remove the meat from the bones and dice. Set aside.

3. To make the sauce, simmer the tomatillos, peppers, onions, bouillon cubes, and broth for about 1 hour. Puree and then strain.

4. Dip the tortillas into hot oil to give them a quick fry and cover to keep warm while you make the enchiladas.

5. Place a small amount of chicken and cheese in the middle of each tortilla and then roll up. Place into a baking dish and cover with the sauce and top with sour cream.

6. Bake at 400°F for 20 minutes. Serve immediately.

LOBSTER A LA NEWBERG

1830, DELMONICO'S, NEW YORK, NEW YORK

The creation of this dish begins with a man named Benjamin J. Wenberg, who was a native of Portland, Maine, and lived in New York City. He was a sea captain who sailed between New York and various Southern ports trading fruit. Captain Wenberg was a fashionable man and often wore a silk cap to dine. He loved good food and frequently dined at Delmonico's at 26th Street and Fifth Avenue as well as their 14th Street location. According to the assistant manager at the time, Arthur Nies, Wenberg didn't invent the dish, but likely picked it up in his travels and introduced it to Delmonico's in 1876 when the captain was about forty years old. In an interview Nies gave to the *New York Herald* in 1910, he said the recipe had its origins at the 26th and Fifth location. He stated that when the dish was made to perfection, it only contained lobster, sweet cream, unsalted butter, French cognac, dry Spanish sherry, and cayenne pepper.

The story goes that when Captain Wenberg was shown to his table one night, he cooked the dish himself and then Charles Delmonico wanted it on his menu. According to Nies, "The dish was first named 'lobster a la Wenberg,' but Mr. Charles Delmonico, or 'Old Charlie,' as he was familiarly known . . . had a quarrel with Ben Wenberg and as the dish had been formally named only a short time before, he inverted the first syllable of the name, and it has ever since been known as 'lobster a la Newberg.'" Wenberg and his younger brother Louis both died on the same day in 1885, he from pneumonia and his brother from consumption. Nies ended the story with, "It is now several years since he passed away, but his favorite dish will continue to tickle the palates of coming generations long after he is forgotten." Another story appeared in the *Buffalo Courier* nine years earlier when correspondent Charles Low wrote, "Mr. Benjamin Wenberg was a habituate of Delmonico's and one of the swells who made the chafing dish popular. When Delmonico put lobster, cooked after his recipe a la Wenberg, the society swell objected to notoriety in this way, so the first syllable was reversed and lobster prepared this way has been a la Newberg ever since."

Chef Charles Ranhofer put his own spin on the recipe and his includes raw egg yolks and Madeira wine instead of sherry and brandy. It has appeared on Delmonico's menus as both "a la Newburg" and "a la Delmonico." It's also interesting that there are also recipes for Clams, Oysters, and Terrapin a la Newberg. In addition, there is a recipe for Lamb Trotters a la Bordelaise Wenberg, but the recipe is not similar to a la Newberg.

For more history on Delmonico's, see the Eggs Benedict recipe.

SERVES 4–6

2–3 pounds steamed lobster meat

4 tablespoons butter

Salt to taste

3 tablespoons Madeira, port, or marsala wine

1½ cups heavy cream

Cayenne pepper to taste

4 large egg yolks, beaten well

1. Cut the lobster into ½-inch pieces.

2. Melt the butter in a saucepan over medium heat. Sprinkle the lobster with salt and warm the lobster meat in the butter over moderate heat for 2 minutes, stirring occasionally. Add the wine and cook for another 2 minutes.

3. Transfer the lobster to a serving bowl and set aside.

4. Add the cream to the wine mixture and increase the heat to medium-high. Boil the mixture until it is reduced to about half.

5. Turn the heat to low and add the cayenne. Whisk in the yolks and cook, whisking constantly, until it registers 140°F, about 3 to 4 minutes.

6. Pour the sauce over the lobster and serve immediately.

BAKED LOBSTER

1946, FISHERMAN'S WHARF INN,
BOOTHBAY HARBOR, MAINE

The Fisherman's Wharf Inn opened in the summer of 1960 and was built on Boothbay Harbor so guests could enjoy the beautiful views. The facility, owned by the Fisherman's Wharf Corporation, contained a restaurant, a twenty-four-room motel, a cocktail lounge, and a gift shop and sporting goods store. In 1971 they advertised, "A different place for your dining pleasure, over the water. Delicious food, all varieties."

This was one of their popular recipes in the 1960s and '70s, but is no longer on the menu. Today you can choose to have your lobster fresh-steamed with melted butter, stuffed with seafood, or shucked.

1 whole live lobster, your choice of weight

Cracker crumbs, enough to cover

Salt to taste

Melted butter, enough to moisten cracker crumbs and for dipping

1. Place the lobster upside side down on a large, clean cutting surface.

2. Steady the lobster with one hand and using a large, heavy chef's knife, pierce the head bluntly and swiftly with the tip of the knife to kill the lobster quickly.

3. From the tip of the knife still in the lobster, bring the knife down along the middle, cutting the lobster in half. Remove the intestinal vein, but leave the tomalley.

4. Crack the claws with a wooden mallet, the back of the heavy chef's knife, or crackers; do not remove the meat.

5. Sprinkle crackers crumbs on the meat, salt as you like, and top with melted butter to moisten the crumbs.

6. Bake at 450°F until the end of the tail is crisp, which takes about 30 minutes.

7. Serve hot with melted butter for dipping.

DEVILED CRAB

1881, WINKLER'S, WILMINGTON, DELAWARE

Winkler's started out as a saloon when German native Louis Winkler emigrated to the United States. He petitioned the State of Delaware to allow him to keep an inn or tavern starting September 1, 1881, at 1419 French Street. In his petition he noted his intention "to sell intoxicating liquors in quantities of less than one quart to be drunk on the premises." In 1888 Winkler bought the saloon from his friend Joseph Stoeckle for $5,500. He died in 1892, but his wife Annie continued to run the saloon.

In 1911 Annie acquired another saloon, owned by James A. Kelly, at the corner of 10th and Shipley Streets. She continued to add to her real estate collection and during the next three years purchased additional lots along French Street and Shipley. In 1918 sons Charles and Harry operated the Winkler Hotel at Shipley and 10th. By 1920 Charles had moved to Philadelphia, and in 1921 Harry was running the Colonial Inn. In 1932 Annie died suddenly, possibly due to a heart condition, at Harry's house and he took over the business. By 1933 the saloon became a restaurant. Harry and his wife Mary ran it and advertised, "Winkler's

lunch hour is a happy hour. Delightful environment, delicious Valley Forge beer." In 1946 the legacy continued when their sons Henry and Louis took over the business.

Longevity of staff was a trademark at Winkler's. Their bartender was Walter Pietchman, who worked there for thirty years when Henry and Louis took over, and their chef, Lawrence Smith, was with them for twenty-six years. Henry Winkler told a newspaper reporter, "We have the best chef in town. For good, straight cooking he can't be beat." One of their most requested recipes was deviled crab.

SERVES 6

2 cups dry bread crumbs

1 cup milk

2 cups crabmeat

Dash of dry mustard

2 teaspoons salt

Dash of cayenne pepper

¼ cup melted butter

6 crab shells or ramekins

Bread crumbs and butter, for topping

1. Combine the bread crumbs and milk in a large bowl and soak for 5 to 10 minutes.

2. Add the crabmeat, mustard, salt, cayenne pepper, and melted butter.

3. Divide the mixture among the crab shells or ramekins. Lightly sprinkle with bread crumbs and dot with butter.

4. Bake at 450°F for 10 minutes or until browned. Serve immediately.

ALLEGHENY MOUNTAIN TROUT

1800s, THE OMNI HOMESTEAD RESORT, HOT SPRINGS, VIRGINIA

Fresh, local trout has been a popular menu item at the Homestead for more than a century and is still served today in the hotel's dining room. While the dish has been updated over the years, the menu has recently featured Sautéed Allegheny Mountain Trout Almondine, which is served with marble potatoes, haricots verts, macerated grapes, and brown butter sauce. The trout served at the Homestead comes from a variety of local sources.

Longtime chef Albert Schnarwyler Jr. lived to be ninety-three and spent over forty of those years as chef at the Homestead. He was born on July 4, 1929, in Lucerne, Switzerland, and began his hospitality career at the Hotel St. Gothard in Zurich and the Schwanen Restaurant in Lucerne. He arrived in America aboard the RMS *Queen Elizabeth* in 1950. Upon arrival he became the sauce cook at the Greenbrier in White Sulphur Springs, West Virginia. He joined the US Army in 1953 and was stationed at Fort Bragg in Fayetteville, North Carolina, where he served as the chief cook, salad maker, and busboy in the general's kitchen.

Schnarwyler later worked for the Park Plaza Hotel in St. Louis, Missouri, and New York's Ambassador Hotel, Gotham Hotel, and Sheraton East Ambassador Hotel. In 1961 he went to Tel Aviv, Israel, to the Sheraton as the executive chef, then returned to the United States in 1962 and became the executive chef for the Homestead in 1963. In 1989 he, along with a North Carolina couple named Ferguson, wrote and published a cookbook titled *Dining at the Homestead.* He retired at the age of seventy-three in 2002.

Todd Owen is the current executive chef and has been cooking for twenty-three years. Some of his staff still remember Albert Schnarwyler when he was the chef. Owen first learned to cook at a vocational school and then attended the Culinary Institute of America for baking and pastry. Eight years ago, he switched from being a pastry chef to cooking. He loves cooking in the historical Homestead and enjoys sneaking down three levels to dabble in the century-old brick oven and play with pastries—time permitting. Chef Todd uses local ingredients when possible and changes some of the items on the menu so that he can offer seasonal fare.

This is Executive Chef Todd Owen's take on the Homestead's trout, which is similar to Chef Schnarwyler's but with a modern flair.

SERVES 6

6 trout fillets, trimmed and deboned

Salt and white pepper to taste

½ cup gluten-free flour blend

1½ cups blanched, sliced almonds

2 tablespoons butter

¼ cup vegetable oil

Brown butter sage sauce (recipe follows)

1. Rinse the trout and pat dry with a towel. Set skin side down on a parchment paper–lined pan and lightly season with salt and white pepper.

2. Using a small sifter, coat the trout with flour, completely covering the flesh.

3. Sprinkle the blanched almonds on top of the floured trout, covering 90 percent of the trout with a single layer of nuts. Refrigerate for 1 hour, allowing the flour

to "glue" the almonds to the trout.

4. Preheat a large cast-iron pan over medium heat. Add the butter and vegetable oil, blending and heating together.

5. Add the trout, almond side down, being careful to gently lay the fillets away from you. The butter oil should not cover the trout, but only come up the sides.

6. Cook the trout for 2 to 3 minutes on the almond side until it is a light golden brown. Flip the trout to skin side down and cook another 2 to 3 minutes on the skin side to crisp.

7. Remove the trout from the pan to a towel-lined plate or a resting screen to allow excess butter oil to drip off. Serve with brown butter sage sauce.

BROWN BUTTER SAGE SAUCE

MAKES 3 CUPS

1 quart heavy cream

8 ounces butter

1 sprig fresh sage

3 sprigs fresh thyme

1 large whole-bulb shallot, peeled and sliced

3 lemons

Salt and white pepper to taste

1. In a heavy-bottomed pot, reduce the cream by half.

2. When the cream is almost done reducing and using another heavy-bottomed saucepot, heat the butter, sage, thyme, and shallots on medium-high heat. Cook until foam disappears and butter solids are dark golden brown.

3. Remove the butter from the heat. Using a whisk, stream in the reduced cream, whisking quickly to emulsify together.

4. Return the pot to the stove on low heat. Add the juice from the lemons and season with salt and white pepper. Do not bring to a boil, as it may "break" the sauce and become oily.

5. Pour the sauce through a fine strainer and hold warm for service.

TROUT AMANDINE

1882, TWIN LAKES INN, TWIN LAKES, COLORADO

This is the Twin Lake Inn's current chef's version of a trout recipe that has been served at this establishment since its beginning. Any trout can be used, but they prefer Ruby Red, when it's in season. For a history of the inn, see the Lamb Bolognese recipe.

SERVES 2

2 (6–8 ounce) trout fillets

Salt and pepper to taste

4 tablespoons butter, divided

1 teaspoon diced shallot

1 teaspoon diced garlic

¼ cup slivered almonds

2 tablespoons lemon juice

2 tablespoons white wine

1 tablespoon chopped fresh parsley

Lemon slices, optional

1. Season the trout fillets with salt and pepper.

2. In a large skillet, melt 2 tablespoons butter over medium heat. Once the butter is bubbling, add the fillets and cook 2 to 3 minutes per side, then remove the fish to a plate to rest.

3. Add the remaining butter, shallots, garlic, and almonds to the skillet. Cook until the almonds are lightly toasted.

4. Add the lemon juice and wine to the pan and let it reduce by half.

5. Top the fish with the sauce, parsley, and lemon slices if desired.

COLUMBIA RIVER SALMON A LA GORGE

1921, COLUMBIA GORGE HOTEL, HOOD RIVER, OREGON

An Oregon lumberman named Simon Benson was a visionary who believed tourism would be the wave of the future for the stunning Columbia River valley back in the 1920s. He also knew that good roads and comfortable accommodations were needed to accomplish his dream. In part, he accomplished that by becoming the first chairman of the Oregon Highway Commission. In May 1921 he told the *Hood River News*, "My main thought is not a profit-making enterprise, but to express my ideas of what a tourist hotel ought to be. . . . I have always contended that before we could expect to attract tourists in numbers, we should be preprepared to entertain them and minister to their physical comfort."

But it was his former chef at the Benson Hotel in Portland, Henry Thiele, who discovered the tract of land where the Columbia Gorge Hotel stands. After Benson sold his Portland hotel, he told Thiele that when he was ready to start his own business to let him know and he would "back him." One day Thiele reached out and said, "Mr. Benson, I have found *the* spot." Benson told him he'd look it over and drove down to the site where the hotel sits today. He told Thiele, "Yes, the location is right," and the deal was done. They built a forty-eight-room hotel on a picturesque site where Meriwether Lewis and William Clark once camped. Chef-owner Henry Thiele delighted his hotel guests with his Columbia River salmon recipes and Hood River apple pie. His dining room had a seating capacity of 600, and the main room on the main floor had oak floors for dancing. The hotel, dubbed "the Waldorf of the West," was the spot for social activity in the Hood River area and a resort for the rich and famous.

Before leaving the Benson Hotel in 1917, Thiele claimed he invented synthetic potatoes and his story was shared in newspapers across the country. It was wartime, and he said his creation was more nourishing and 50 percent cheaper. His recipe included water, wheat flour, potatoes, split peas, and lard that was molded into potato shapes and boiled, mashed, baked, or fried. He noted, "I furnished the substitute for potatoes when potatoes were scarce, now when wheat is high and needed in the war, and potatoes are cheaper, I furnish a substitute for wheat bread, made principally of potatoes." Thiele was such an excellent chef that even James Beard remembered him. In 1983 Beard recalled, "My first adventure with tarragon, which resulted in a serious case of love at first bite, came when I was very young and tasted a bearnaise sauce from the hands of Henri Thiele. He was then working at the old Benson Hotel in Portland. I subsequently followed him to many different spots at which he reigned as chef, because in all my experience, no one has ever made a bearnaise equal to his."

SERVES 4–6

6½-pound salmon fillets

2 teaspoons salt

1 lemon, sliced thin

1 small onion, slice thin

1 bay leaf

Special Sauce a la Gorge

Paprika, parsley, and lemon slices, for garnish

1. Place the salmon fillets in a stockpot and add just enough water to cover. Add the salt, lemon slices, onion, and bay leaf. Cover and slowly bring to a boil.

2. Remove the salmon from the pot and place on a serving platter or individual plates. Add some sauce and garnish with a sprinkle of paprika, parsley, and lemon slices.

SPECIAL SAUCE A LA GORGE
MAKES 2½ CUPS

2 cups white sauce (see recipe for béchamel on page 33)

3 dashes Louisiana hot sauce

½ cup grated cheddar cheese

Combine all the ingredients in a saucepan and heat over low heat until blended.

CHICKEN-FRIED STEAK

1910, CATTLEMEN'S STEAKHOUSE, OKLAHOMA CITY, OKLAHOMA

Chicken-fried steak has been a long-standing tradition and is one of Cattlemen's Steak-house's signature dishes. For a history of the restaurant, see the Lamb Fries recipe.

SERVES 1

1 cup flour

1 teaspoon white pepper

1 teaspoon MSG

1 4-ounce cubed beef steak

Whole milk, for coating

Vegetable oil, for frying

1. Combine the flour, pepper, and MSG into a shallow pan.

2. Dredge the cubed steak in the seasoned flour. Shake off excess flour. Dip into milk.

3. Place the steak back into the seasoned flour. Press it with the heel of your hand until the meat is thin and evenly coated with breading. (Do not discard leftover flour or milk.)

4. Heat a skillet, preferably cast iron, over medium-high heat. Add enough oil to barely coat the bottom. This is pan-friend, not deep-fried.

5. Once the oil is shimmering, add the steak and cook about 5 minutes or until golden brown. Turn the steak and cook for about another 5 minutes until this side is golden brown. If the meat is thick, it will need to cook longer.

6. When the meat is cooked, remove it to a plate and keep warm.

7. To make the gravy, use the small amount of oil that should still be in the bottom of the skillet. Reduce heat to low heat and stir in 1–2 tablespoons of the seasoned flour to make a roux. Cook at low heat for 5 minutes until roux is light brown.

8. Gradually add the leftover milk used for dredging (about 1–2 tablespoons) to the roux and stir until thickened. You can gently add a little more milk at a time to reach your preferred consistency.

9. Place the pan gravy onto a platter. Gently lay the chicken-fried steak onto the gravy—this keeps the top crust from getting soggy so it remains crispy while eating. Enjoy!

CORNISH PASTY

1906, GAMERS CONFECTIONERY AND CAFÉ, BUTTE, MONTANA

J. Fred Gamer moved from Helena, Montana, where he grew up, to Butte to run his father's Butte Gamer Shoe Company store in 1889. Fred decided that he wanted his own store, so in 1906 he and his wife Sophie opened Gamers' Schwab Company, Confectionery, Ice Cream and Fancy Ices at 133 West Park. The company included Fred, M. A. Gamer, and Dr. J. M. Scanland and offered fresh-made candies, ice cream, frozen puddings, and a variety of other items. They did well and eventually sold the business in 1944. Fred offered this old-world Cornish meat pie that the English, Welsh, and Irish immigrants appreciated.

SERVES 6

1 pound sirloin tip beef

3 potatoes, peeled and diced

3 green onions, diced

Salt and pepper to taste

1 cup lard or shortening

1 ounce butter

4 cups flour

2 teaspoons salt

Pinch of baking powder

Cold water

1 egg

1 tablespoon cream

Owner J. Fred Gamer as he appeared in the November 1950 Montana Standard

1. To make the filling, cut the steak into small cubes and add it along with the potatoes, onions, and salt and pepper to a large bowl. Mix well and set aside.

2. To make the crust, place the lard, butter, flour, salt, and baking powder into a bowl. Using a pastry blender or two knives, cut the lard and butter into the flour until it resembles pea-size crumbles. Add enough cold water, a tablespoon at a time, to form a stiff ball.

3. Roll out the dough onto a floured surface to ⅛-inch thick. Cut into 6 circles, about 6 inches wide.

4. Divide the filling into 6 portions and place each portion into the center of each dough circle. Moisten the edges of each one and press them in half. Seal the edges with a fork.

5. Beat the egg and cream together and brush over the pasties. Make a hole in the center for the steam to escape and bake at 425°F for 1 hour.

SOUR SCHMORRBRATEN (SAUERBRATEN)

1904, CLUB CONTINENTAL IN THE JEFFERSON HOTEL, ST. LOUIS, MISSOURI

See the Rice Mangalais with Curry Sauce recipe for the history of the Jefferson Hotel. Chef Otto Klopfer shared many of his classic recipes, like this one, in the St. Louis newspapers.

SERVES 6–8

1 roast (about 4 pounds)

Salt and pepper to taste

1 onion, peeled and sliced

1 carrot, chopped

1 celery stalk, chopped

1 leek, washed and chopped

2 parsley sprigs

2 bay leaves

1 thyme sprig

2 cloves

4 cups white vinegar

2 ounces butter

2 tablespoons flour

1½ quarts beef broth

3 tomatoes, chopped

Here's a Palate Pleaser!

Chef Otto Klopfer of Hotel Jefferson.

Tells of a New Popular Salad

OLE KING COLE would have been a merrier ole soul if he'd had Shel-Roni served with his truffles. Chef Otto Klopfer of the Hotel Jefferson has royally expressed his culinary art in Shel-Roni Bagration.

1. Rub the roast with salt and pepper. Place the roast and the vegetables, herbs, and vinegar into a glass bowl and cover. Refrigerate for 36 to 48 hours.

2. Remove the meat and drain and dry it. Strain the marinade and reserve 1 cup.

3. Heat a large stockpot over medium-high heat and melt the butter. Fry the beef until golden brown on all sides. Remove the meat and set aside.

4. Add the flour to the pot and cook for 1 minute. Add the reserved marinade and the broth and put the beef in the pot. Bring to a boil, then add the tomatoes and reduce heat to a simmer. Cover and cook for about 3 hours or until tender.

5. Remove the meat and place on a cutting board to rest.

6. Reduce the sauce over high heat until thickened to your liking. Taste for seasoning.

7. Slice the meat thin and serve with the gravy and egg noodles.

SPAGHETTI AND MEATBALLS

1900, RALPH'S ITALIAN RESTAURANT, PHILADELPHIA, PENNSYLVANIA

On July 17, 1893, Francesco "Frank" Dispigno arrived in New York City with his family and headed to Philadelphia. After settling in South Philly, Francesco recognized his booming neighborhood was perfect for a small restaurant. He gathered all his savings and rented a building at 901 Montrose Street where he and his wife Catherine opened their Italian restaurant in 1900 that was affectionately called Ralph's, after their son. Frank's idea was a hit, and they eventually outgrew their location. By 1908 Francesco and Catherine purchased a boardinghouse on South 9th Street where the reputation of Ralph's Italian Restaurant would continue to exceed expectations.

In 1918 Frank retired and his son Ralph, who was a visionary much like his father, took over the business. In 1922 *La Libera Parola*, an Italian newspaper in Philadelphia, wrote this about the restaurant: "The old and renowned restaurant . . . directed with intellect of love by the young Mr. Rafaele, and the meeting place of the most chosen class of our compatriots, both for the exquisite food, who knows how to prepare that for the impeccable service that is practiced there. The Italian families, we are sure, on Sundays and other holidays and during the evenings of next winter, will go to take their meals . . . sparing yourself the hassle of cooking in the memorable rounds."

A 1947 ad in the *Philadelphia Inquirer* noted, "Famous for its Italian food since 1900. Fine beverages served. Air conditioned for your comfort." The backbone of Ralph's has always been family, and as Ralph and his wife Mary's kids grew, they learned how to run the business based on the same values that made the brand successful. Ralph's is still family owned and serves the same spaghetti and meatballs recipe that Francesco served when he opened so long ago.

ITALIAN MEAT SAUCE (THEY CALL IT GRAVY)

SERVES 10–12

1 large Spanish onion, peeled and chopped

6 to 8 large garlic cloves, minced

1 cup extra-virgin olive oil

½ pound ground beef

½ pound ground pork

3 (28-ounce) cans tomatoes, crushed by hand

1 bunch fresh basil, chopped

1½ tablespoons salt

1 teaspoon black pepper

1 teaspoon crushed fennel seed

½ cup chopped fresh parsley

3 tablespoons tomato paste

1. Sauté the onion and garlic with the olive oil in a 6-quart saucepot for 3 minutes. Add the ground meats and sauté until the meat is browned, stirring constantly.

2. Add the tomatoes, then all the remaining ingredients. Bring to a boil, then lower the heat and simmer for 1½ hours, stirring occasionally.

RALPH'S ITALIAN MEATBALLS

MAKES 10–15 MEATBALLS

½ loaf Italian bread, dampened in water

1½ pounds ground beef

1½ pounds ground pork

2 large eggs

5 large garlic cloves, minced

½ cup grated Pecorino Romano cheese

1 tablespoon salt

¾ tablespoon black pepper

¾ cup chopped fresh parsley

4 cups vegetable oil

1. Squeeze the excess water from the bread and add all the ingredients except the oil to a large mixing bowl. Use your hands to ensure everything is well mixed. Roll into meatballs a bit larger than a golf ball.

2. Heat the oil in a large pan on a medium flame. When the oil is hot (about 350°F), gently add 6 or 7 meatballs to the pan, ensuring there is room between them to cook evenly. Fry for about 3 minutes, then rotate and do the same to the uncooked side.

3. Place the cooked meatballs on a brown paper bag to drain excess oil.

4. Boil your favorite pasta and drain well. Top with some of the meat sauce and add meatballs. Sprinkle with Parmesan cheese, if you like.

SWEDISH COLLOPS (SWEDISH BEEF STEW)

1918, NORTON HOTEL, DETROIT, MICHIGAN

Charles Norton opened the four-story, 250-room Norton Hotel on the northeast corner of Griswold Street and Jefferson Avenue on June 19, 1918. An ad for the hotel boasted that it had "a wonderful view of the Detroit River, the Canadian frontier and the city." It also had a restaurant that sat 200 in a dining room that offered views overlooking the Detroit River that were unmatched at the time it was built.

It wasn't until the 1940s that A Bit of Sweden opened in the Norton. Swedish-born Eric Lundahl worked at Schweize's for a while and in 1941 was running his own Swedish restaurant in Detroit. His restaurant, A Bit of Sweden, began on Bates Street and offered a traditional smorgasbord as well as steaks, seafood, lobster, and frog legs. Around September 1942 the restaurant moved into the Norton Hotel. In 1945 Lundahl advertised, "Skal. Smorgasbord. The only one served on natural ice. Here eating is more than a routine necessity—it is a pleasant adventure. Complete luncheons and dinner. Choice liquors. 'If your wife cannot cook, do not divorce her, bring her to: A Bit of Sweden. Famed for good in the Norton Hotel. Airconditioned.'" Lundahl often traveled to Sweden to make sure he "didn't lose his touch" with old-world recipes and customs. This beef stew recipe is one of his traditional dishes that was served at the hotel.

SERVES 4

2¾ pounds round steak

2 tablespoons butter

¾ tablespoon salt

¾ tablespoon pepper

2–3 whole allspice

2 bay leaves

1 large onion, peeled and sliced

Water or weak stock

2 tablespoons flour

1½ cups cream

Salt and pepper to taste

1. Cut the round steak into 1-inch cubes. Heat a deep pot over medium-high heat and melt the butter.

2. Sear the beef on all sides. Add seasonings, onion, and enough water or stock to cover. Simmer for 2 hours.

3. Strain the juice into a small bowl and place the drained meat into another bowl to keep warm. Set both aside.

4. Skim some fat from the juice, add it back to the pan, and heat over medium heat. Add the flour and 7 tablespoons of water to the pan and stir until browned.

5. Gradually add the remaining meat juice, then add the cream and cook for 8 to 10 minutes.

6. Season with salt and pepper to taste and pour over the meat.

SWEDISH MEATBALLS

1885, LUTSEN RESORT, LUTSEN, MINNESOTA

The story of Lutsen Resort began in 1881 when Charles Axel Nelson ("C.A.A.") emigrated from Sweden to Duluth, Minnesota, when he was eighteen. He soon married Anna Peterson, also a Swedish native, and worked as a captain of a fishing tug. He frequently cast his nets near rivers along the North Shore, and the cove at the mouth of the Poplar River was his favorite spot. C.A.A.'s skill as a fisherman caught the attention of the A. Booth Packing Company office in Duluth, and the company offered him his own boat and fishing supplies on credit if he would become one of their suppliers. He agreed, and in 1885 filed a homestead for 160 acres at the mouth of the Poplar River for twelve dollars.

Anna remained in Duluth while her husband built a shanty, followed by a log cabin, on the hill and a fish house and dock. The next year he was joined by his wife and their infant son, Carl. They found their new home comfortable but quite remote, with their closest neighbors ten miles down the shore. Hard work was in store and they also logged their land with a team of oxen, hunted and traded in furs, did potato farming, and fished as far away as Isle Royale. Some of C.A.A.'s exploits seem mythical, like when he rowed a boat seventy miles from Two Harbors to Lutsen without stopping. In 1888 his parents and brothers Gust and Alfred joined his family from Sweden.

Visitors to the region seeking shelter soon discovered hospitality at the Nelsons' home. New settlers to the region such as hunters, fishermen, mineral explorers, loggers, and timber cruisers arrived by boat in the rough Lake Superior waters, or came overland on trails via wagon, sleigh, horseback, dog team, or simply on foot. At first, C.A.A. and Anna put up lodgers in their home and in the hay loft of their barn. Anna handled all the work involved in providing for their visitors, including cooking hearty Swedish fare for hungry guests and carrying water up from the lake for cooking and cleaning. C.A.A. began a guide service for the fishermen and hunters, and word of the plentiful supply of moose, bear, and fish soon began to spread to the Twin Cities, Chicago, and beyond. In reality, the Lutsen House was merely the second floor of the large house that C.A.A. built in 1893. Often, their own children were displaced to make room for their guests. To take care of the needs of the fledgling settlement, a small town sprang up at the homestead site, including a post office, general store, and town hall. The Nelsons' family grew as well, with daughters Ida, Hilda, and Elsie and sons Edwin, George, and Oscar joining their first-born son, Carl.

By 1952 the current Scandinavian-style lodge was built, using mostly white pine logs taken from the Gunflint Trail area. Designed by Edwin Lundie, a Scotsman and architect who loved carved wood and Swedish design, the dining room's rustic ambience brings the flavor of the North Shore indoors. The fireplace in the dining room, like the massive fireplace in the main reception area, is built from stone taken from the area. The carvings throughout the lodge were accomplished by local craftsmen. Lutsen Resort was the first place to serve bluefin, herring with the skin removed, and visitors still enjoy traditional Swedish baked goods like pies and breads. These meatballs can be enjoyed as an appetizer with a side of caraway crème fraîche and lingonberry preserves or served over mashed potatoes or wild rice with sauce on the side and your favorite vegetable!

MAKES 64 APPETIZER-SIZE OR
32 DINNER-SIZE MEATBALLS

¼ **pound bread crumbs**

½ **cup milk**

1½ **ounces butter**

¾ **cup finely chopped yellow onion**

1 **pound ground pork**

2 **pounds ground beef**

⅛ **teaspoon ground nutmeg**

⅛ **teaspoon ground allspice**

⅛ **teaspoon ground cardamom**

¼ **teaspoon ground caraway seeds**

½ **tablespoon kosher salt**

¼ **tablespoon black pepper**

2 **cups water**

Mushroom gravy (recipe follows)

Caraway crème fraîche (recipe follows)

1. Combine the bread crumbs and milk in a large mixing bowl. Set aside and allow to soften.

2. Melt the butter in a small saucepan over low heat and add the onion. Turn off heat and allow to cool.

3. Place the onion, pork, beef, spices, salt, and pepper in a mixing bowl and mix for 2 minutes. Add the moistened bread crumbs and beat for another 4 minutes on low speed, but don't overmix.

4. Refrigerate the mixture for 1 hour.

5. Once chilled, make 1-ounce balls for appetizer portions or 2-ounce balls for dinners and place on a baking tray. Pour water into the baking tray and bake for 15 minutes at 325°F.

6. Drain the water and let the meatballs cool.

7. To serve the dish, warm the meatballs in the mushroom gravy and serve with a side of caraway crème fraîche.

MUSHROOM GRAVY
MAKES ABOUT 3 TO 3½ CUPS

2½ ounces butter

½ pound chopped wild mushroom blend

1 tablespoon finely chopped shallot

½ tablespoon chopped garlic

2½ ounces flour

½ tablespoon fresh thyme

2 cups demi-glace

½ cup heavy cream

½ tablespoon black pepper

½ tablespoon kosher salt

½ cup sour cram

1. Melt the butter in a pot over medium heat and add mushrooms, shallot, and garlic. Cook until the mushrooms are tender.

2. Add the flour and cook for 5 minutes on low flame to create a roux. Add the thyme and cook for 1 more minute.

3. Add the demi-glace and bring to a low boil, being sure to keep the heat on low. Cook for 10 minutes, stirring frequently.

4. Add the heavy cream, black pepper, and salt and cook for 5 minutes.

5. Turn off the heat. Add the sour cream and mix well.

CARAWAY CRÈME FRAÎCHE
MAKES ABOUT 1 CUP

½ cup sour cream

½ cup heavy whipping cream

½ tablespoon fresh dill

1 tablespoon toasted caraway seeds

Combine all the ingredients in a bowl and mix well by hand.

PRIME RIB

1952, BROWN PALACE HOTEL, DENVER, COLORADO

Ohio native Henry Cordes Brown stopped in Denver in 1860 and later purchased several acres of land in a "remote part of the West." To make this happen, he sold the remaining portion of his land on what was called "Capitol Hill." After profitable sales, Brown spared no expense in building his new hotel. He hired Denver architect Frank E. Edbrooke and work on the hotel began in 1888, when the Wild West was in full swing. Edbrooke designed Brown's hotel in the Italian Renaissance style, using Colorado red granite and Arizona sandstone for the building's exterior. Artesian wells, 720 feet deep, were dug beneath the hotel to provide water and are still used today. When his hotel was completed, Brown had spent a staggering $1.1 million, in addition to $400,000 more to furnish it.

The Brown Palace Hotel is a place where guests have been spoiled since its opening on August 12, 1892. The hotel originally had 400 guest rooms, which rented for between one dollar and four dollars per night. There were no restaurants in the hotel, but it did have two banquet halls, a ladies' ordinary (lounge), and the Grand Salon. The lobby offered a smoking room, a men's bar, and a ladies' waiting room, along with eighteen stores. The hotel's

interior contains the country's first atrium lobby with balconies rising eight stories high, surrounded by cast-iron railings and ornate grillwork panels. For reasons unknown, two of the grillwork panels were installed, and still remain, upside down. For a finishing touch, artist James Whitehouse carved twenty-six stone medallions, each depicting a Rocky Mountain animal. These can still be seen today between the seventh-floor windows. The lobby floors, Grand Salon, and eighth-floor ballroom were made of imported Mexican white onyx. The hotel contains 12,400 surface feet of onyx—the most ever used in one building at the time.

The main dining hall for hotel guests, on the eighth floor, was two stories high and offered a beautiful panoramic view of the Rocky Mountains. The hotel kitchens were also on that floor, and just above them were the servants' dining room, staff dressing rooms, and lavatories. The menus were as lavish as the hotel itself and included dishes such as broiled lake trout with anchovy sauce and lamb chops a la Nelson. Prime ribs of beef, as they were called in the nineteenth century, were often served in American restaurants, but some businesses became known for their version and it became their signature dish. The Brown Palace started offering ribs of beef very early on. Even though the original restaurant was on the upper floors of the hotel, it was later replaced by others on the ground floor. The Ship's Tavern opened in 1934 and has been serving the same prime rib recipe that was created in 1952.

SERVES 4-6

1 (3-rib) uncooked prime rib roast

Equal parts salt, black pepper, granulated garlic, thyme, onion powder, and rosemary

1. Place the meat in an oven-ready roasting pan. Remove excess blood by patting dry.

2. Blend the seasonings together and then generously coat the top of the roast with the mix, as much or as little as you like.

3. Blast the roast in a 400°F oven for 20 minutes. After 20 minutes, lower the temperature to 275°F and cook to an internal temperature of 101°F.

4. Let rest for 15 minutes before cutting or hold until service time.

SONORAN SPICE BRISKET

1965, WHITE STALLION RANCH, TUCSON, ARIZONA

Chef Judy of the White Stallion Ranch came up with this recipe, along with many of the others that she still uses on the ranch to this day. For a history of the ranch, see the Breakfast Ride Potatoes recipe.

SERVES 10–12

½ **cup garlic powder**

½ **cup chili powder**

½ **cup paprika**

½ **cup dried oregano**

½ **cup salt**

¼ **cup dried coriander**

2 **tablespoons ground cumin**

1 **teaspoon pepper**

1 **brisket (6–7 pounds)**

4–5 **cups water**

1. Combine all the ingredients, except the brisket and water, in a bowl and blend well.

2. Rub the mixture all over the meat. Place the meat in a pan and add the water.

3. Bake at 250°F in a convection oven or 350°F in a regular oven for 4 to 6 hours depending on size.

4. When tender, remove the brisket from the pan and allow it to sit, covered with foil, for about 20 minutes so the juices will be absorbed back into the meat.

5. Slice and serve.

PRICKLY PEAR MARGARITA

1990, WHITE STALLION RANCH, TUCSON, ARIZONA

Prickly pear cactuses grow wild all over southern Arizona, and people have been using their fruits and leaves for generations to create recipes. This drink was created by Michael True.

MAKES 1 DRINK

2 ounces margarita mix

2 ounces tequila

¼ ounce triple sec

¾ ounce prickly pear syrup

1 ounce 7-Up

Combine all the ingredients and stir to blend. Serve over crushed ice in a salted-rim glass.

HUNGARIAN GOULASH

1937, SUN VALLEY RESORT, SUN VALLEY, IDAHO

Count Felix Schaffgotsch was hired by Union Pacific Railroad chairman Averell Harriman to find the perfect spot for a grand American ski resort in Idaho. Upon reaching the Wood River valley, the count was inspired by the area and wired his employer, saying, "This combines more delightful features than any place I have ever seen in Switzerland, Austria, or the U.S. for a winter resort." Harriman agreed and the Sun Valley Lodge was completed in December of 1936.

Realizing that one hotel doesn't make a resort, Sun Valley opened another spacious hostelry in 1938 called the Challenger Inn after Union Pacific's passenger trains. It's now known as the Sun Valley Inn. It was built to resemble a Tyrolean mountain village, which is the alpine region at the meeting point of Austria, Switzerland, and Italy. The hotel was based on drawings by Ernst Fegte, the German set designer of the first movie shot in Sun Valley, *I Met Him in Paris,* starring resort regular Claudette Colbert. Its different facades were painted by American artist Walt Kuhn to enhance the illusion of a classic Austrian village street, when inside it is all one building.

The Ram Restaurant is one of the "sections" of this village-like building. The Ram opened in 1938, making it Sun Valley's oldest restaurant, and had a strong Austrian theme right down to the long-stemmed wine-pourers imported from Vienna by Count Schaffgotsch. The restaurant serves traditional Alpine-influenced dishes, and you can take your tastebuds on a historic culinary journey with the nightly "Heritage Menu." Items include pork ten-

derloin schnitzel and this 1966 Hungarian goulash that's been resurrected from the restaurant's long and storied culinary tradition. This dish has multiple components that include paprika-braised beef, spaetzle, mushrooms, honey carrots, and spinach. See the "Sides and Vegetables" section for the honey carrots, sherried mushrooms, and spaetzle recipes.

SERVES 4

1 boneless short rib or chuck flap (about 3 pounds)

Salt and pepper to taste

½ cup black peppercorns

1 cup whole, peeled garlic cloves

4 ounces fresh thyme

6 large onions, sliced thin

1 cup Hungarian paprika

3 quarts beef stock

4 cups white wine

Goulash sauce

Handful of fresh spinach

Honey carrots

Sherried mushrooms

Spaetzle

1. Season the meat with salt and pepper. Bake in a 475°F oven for 20 minutes, or until all sides are browned. Remove from the oven and reduce the temperature to 300°F.

2. Place the peppercorns, garlic, thyme, and half of the onions in the bottom of a large baking dish. Place the meat on top of the mixture and cover with paprika. Cover the meat with the remaining onions.

3. Bring the beef stock and wine to a boil and pour over the meat. Seal the top of the dish with plastic wrap and then aluminum foil. Place the meat in the oven to cook for 4 hours (or pressure cooker for 1 hour).

4. Remove from the oven and let the meat cool, reserving the braising liquid for the sauce. Strain the cooking particles out of the liquid.

5. When cooled, cut the meat into bite-size pieces and set aside while you make the sauce, honey carrots, sherried mushrooms, and spaetzle batter.

6. When everything is ready, add a little bit of oil to a pan over medium heat. Once heated, add the honey carrots, sherried mushrooms, and meat. When they are heated through, add the sauce.

7. Cook again until heated through. Remove from the heat and add a handful of fresh spinach to wilt.

8. In a separate pan, heat up a little bit of oil. Add the spaetzle batter and cook until a light golden brown.

9. Place the spaetzle around the outer edge of a serving platter and add the goulash to the middle. Enjoy!

GOULASH SAUCE

Strained braising liquid

1 cup tomato juice

1 cup rice flour

1. Add the tomato juice to the braising liquid and bring to a boil over high heat.

2. Add the rice flour a little at a time and stir until desired thickness.

3. Set aside until ready to assemble the dish.

LAMB SHANKS

1919, THE MARTIN HOTEL, WINNEMUCCA, NEVADA

The Martin Hotel, on the corner of Railroad and Melarkey Streets, was originally a dwelling built in 1878 by Frank Naramore, who operated the Railroad Feed and Sale Stables on the same block. In the fall of 1915, French natives Elise Henri and Augustine A. Martin, along with their two sons, Alexis and A. René, arrived in Winnemucca. The Martins had met and married in San Francisco, where they lived until the 1906 earthquake. On December 25, 1915, they held a grand opening for the Martin Restaurant & Bar. The restaurant occupied half of Pasquale's 1908 stone structure, and Pasquale's Uptown Grocery occupied the other half. In addition to the Martin Restaurant & Bar, they also ran a rooming house on the corner called the Martin Hotel. In 1917 Elise Henri was diagnosed with kidney disease, so Alexis took the family back to San Francisco and sold his business interests to his partner, Martin Arbonies.

A few people owned the business over the years, but in 1956 Syl and Rosie Uriguen purchased the Martin Hotel. According to the current owner, John Arant, Rosie created their signature lamb shank recipe.

SERVES 4–6

6 pounds lamb shanks

¼ cup Lamb Spice (recipe follows)

1½ tablespoons Prairie Dust Seasoning (recipe follows)

1½ teaspoons chopped rosemary

1⅔ cups Italian red wine

5¾ cups water

¾ cup chopped garlic

⅓ cup chicken stock

1. Place the lamb shanks in a large sauté pan and sprinkle with the seasonings and rosemary.

2. Cook in a 350°F oven for 1 hour, uncovered.

3. Add the wine, water, chopped garlic, and stock. Cover with foil or a lid and cook for an additional 2 hours, or until tender.

4. Serve with mashed potatoes, vegetables of your choice, French bread, and red wine.

LAMB SPICE

MAKES ABOUT ½ CUP

4 tablespoons salt

2 tablespoons freshly ground black pepper

2 tablespoons garlic powder

1 tablespoon rosemary, or "when you can just smell the rosemary, it's just right"

Blend all of the ingredients together and store in a container.

PRAIRIE DUST SEASONING

MAKES ¼ CUP

4 teaspoons freshly ground black pepper

4 teaspoons garlic powder

4 teaspoons salt

Blend all of the ingredients together and store in a container.

LAMB BOLOGNESE

1882, TWIN LAKES INN, TWIN LAKES, COLORADO

The town of Twin Lakes began as a mining camp called Dayton. In 1877 and 1878 it was listed in Colorado business entries as "Dayton—Miners' camp on the border of Twin Lakes . . . five miles from Granite. Hotel and Supplies: S.M. Derry," who was Samuel Derry. In February 1879 Leadville's *Daily Chronicle* reported, "Twin Lakes is the most delightful summer resort in Colorado, attracting every year hundreds of visitors, and situated about ten miles from Leadville." In May they wrote, "In another month a village of tents will spring up about Twin Lakes, one of the most attractive resorts in the world." They noted that by the summer there would be a good hotel and other comfort features. By 1881 a hotel was operated by "Captain Stiles," the Lakeside House was owned by George Fisher, and the Inter-Laken Hotel was opened by John Staley.

The current Twin Lakes Inn began around 1882 when Albert Wolff operated Wolff's Hotel. He kept it until 1883 and then in 1884 Wisconsin native Mrs. Maggie Webber took it over. She kept the hotel until 1903, but after 1888 it's not clear what its name was. When Mrs. Mary King took over the hotel about July 1903, it was called Twin Peaks. Mary's husband was a miner who was often out of town, but kept her happy by naming a mine after her called the Mary King. She was a good businesswoman, but one day in October 1903 she unknowingly bought some "hot" sheep. Two men named Foxhall and Chisholm stole several sheep from

a nearby pasture and Chisholm sold his twelve to Mary, who used them to make dinners for her patrons. There is no mention of the story other than that.

News arrived in September 1904 in Twin Lakes that the Twin Peaks' former owner Maggie Webber had passed away. The local paper reported, "Mrs. Webber was one of our oldest residents and ran the Twin Peaks Hotel during staging days. She was widely known in the state and highly respected for her good qualities."

In 1906 Mrs. King hired an extra cook and installed a new cookstove to handle the "rush" of visitors to the area who enjoyed fishing for speckled trout. In 1908 she hired Mrs. Mary Sims to be her "culinary artist." After the death of her son in 1911, Mrs. King took some time away from the business and Mrs. T. W. Martin ran the hotel. By 1923 Mrs. King was back at the Twin Peaks. The business has had a few more owners over the years, and today it's known as the Twin Lakes Inn. This establishment, under various owners and chefs, has been serving lamb since the early days. This is their signature version.

SERVES 3-4

½ **pound ground Colorado lamb**

½ **cup chopped white onion**

¾ **cup chopped celery**

¾ **cup chopped carrots**

1 **cup red wine**

1½ **cups canned chopped tomatoes with juice**

1 **teaspoon basil**

1 **teaspoon oregano**

1 **teaspoon thyme**

½ **teaspoon red pepper flakes**

1 **cup milk**

Salt and pepper to taste

1½ **pounds linguine, cooked**

Parmesan cheese to taste

1. Cook the ground lamb in a pot over medium-high heat until it loses its red color. Drain the grease and return the lamb to the pot.

2. Add the onions, celery, and carrots and cook over medium heat until almost tender.

3. Add the red wine and tomatoes and let it reduce for about 15 minutes. Bring it to a boil and then reduce heat and let simmer for 1½ to 2 hours.

4. Add the milk and continue to simmer for 1 hour. Add salt and pepper to taste.

5. Toss the pasta with some sauce and then place in a pasta bowl and top with fresh Parmesan cheese.

MARINATED PORK CHOPS

1958, THE EMBERS, MT. PLEASANT, MICHIGAN

Clarence Tuma graduated from nearby Central Michigan University (CMU) in 1950 with the intent of being an athletic coach. However, food was his destiny and he worked his way through college as a student chef in the CMU dorms. When he was offered a job as a food purchasing agent at CMU, he gave up the coaching idea. He later became assistant director for food services at the university and opened his restaurant in 1958 with Norman "Norm" LaBelle.

Embers staff (left to right): Catering Mgr. Ed Tuma, Kitchen Superintendant Tertia Fabian, Owner Clarence Tuma, Day Chef Norm Tuma, Head Chef Paul Strickler, and Business Mgr. Keith Charters, 1970.

Clarence once told a reporter that the restaurant came to be "over a cup of coffee" between him and Norm. The *Detroit Free Press* reported in 1961, "The ebullient pair, Norm and Clarence, have ingeniously made the Embers a Midwest show place. The intimate design of casual elegance is evidenced in the entrance foyer covered in pigskin tile, panels of Indonesian Batik laminated in plastic—are especially striking features. No dressed-up rhetoric could compliment the succulent food—and the Embers cocktail lounge maintains the high standard of excellence for which it is famous." By 1963 they were known for their one-pound charbroiled pork chop, the restaurant's fine-dining experience, and excellent service. They also specialized in charcoal-broiled food, prime rib, Caesar salad, and a seven-compartment relish tray.

After being in business for ten years, Clarence said, "This combination is our secret to fine and distinctive dining. Our quality food, personable hospitality, and warm surroundings are well known all over. Unlike most restaurants, we make our own dressings and sauces. Our most talked about origination is our peas and peanuts relish. I sometimes receive a dozen letters a week from all parts of the country asking for this recipe. Unfortunately, we cannot let it out." The relish tray also included cucumbers in sour cream and marinated herring.

Diners who had room after their meal were tempted by a cart "heaped" with homemade pastries that came to each table after dinner, including pecan, apple, and lemon meringue pies, cheesecake, cherry tarts, and devil's food cake. Their Angel Pies were probably the most well-known and liked and included chocolate, caramel, lemon, or strawberry in a nut meringue crust. They also offered delicious main dishes like these pork chops.

SERVES 6

2 cups soy sauce

1 cup water

½ cup brown sugar

1 tablespoon dark molasses

1 teaspoon salt

6 (1-pound) center-cut bone-in pork chops

1 tablespoon dry mustard

¼ cup water

1 cup brown sugar

14 ounces ketchup

12 ounces chili sauce

1. Place the soy sauce, water, brown sugar, molasses, and salt into a bowl. Stir to combine and dissolve the sugar.

2. Place the pork chops, bone side up, in an ovenproof glass baking dish and cover with the marinade. Marinate overnight in the refrigerator.

3. Remove from the refrigerator and cover with aluminum foil. Bake in a 375°F oven for about 2 hours or until tender.

4. To make the sauce, combine the mustard and water in a heavy-duty saucepan and stir to blend until there are no lumps. Turn the heat on to medium-low and add the remaining ingredients. Bring to a slight boil, then remove from the heat and set aside.

5. Once the chops are tender, remove them from the oven and dip them in the sauce. Bake, uncovered, for another 30 minutes at 350°F or until slightly glazed.

6. Remove the chops from the oven and keep warm until ready to grill.

7. Place the chops on the grill and cook for about 15 minutes, but do not allow them to get black.

STUFFED PEPPERS, CREOLE STYLE

1941, OLD SOUTHERN TEA ROOM, VICKSBURG, MISSISSIPPI

The Old Southern Tea Room was opened in 1941 by Mary McCay and served classic Southern favorites like fried chicken, country ham, shrimp gumbo, hot biscuits, and corn pudding. Mary's customers were greeted by waitresses who were dressed in colorful costumes and served all of her specialties from her home kitchen made by her own cook. Sadly, the business was destroyed by a fire in 1987. Mary put her Southern spin on this classic recipe by making it Creole style.

SERVES 4-6

8 medium-size green bell peppers

2 onions, chopped

1 (14.5-ounce) can tomatoes, drained

2 cups bread crumbs, plus more for topping

2 tablespoons butter, room temperature

½ cup chopped cooked ham

Salt and pepper to taste

1. Chop two of the peppers and place into a medium bowl. Remove the tops from the remaining 6 peppers, clean, and scald in boiling water.

2. Add the onions, tomatoes, bread crumbs, butter, ham, and salt and pepper to the chopped peppers. Stir to mix well and stuff into the whole peppers.

3. Sprinkle with some bread crumbs and bake for about 40 minutes at 350°F until peppers are tender.

NAVAJO TACOS

1925, ZION LODGE, SPRINGDALE, UTAH

It was 1923 when the Union Pacific Railroad chose architect Gilbert Stanley Underwood to design their new structure in Springdale, Utah. Their decision was based on the fact that he had already created a number of other buildings for them in the Grand Canyon and Bryce Canyon. Utah Parks Company designed the main lodge building that was inviting and exuded warmth to preserve the natural beauty of the area. Underwood used 265,000 board feet of lumber brought down from the plateau by the Cable Mountain Draw Works. The lodge was completed in May 1925, and was later complemented by a series of stand-alone cabins nestled nearby.

References to Indian fried bread and Navajo/Indian fry bread are pretty much the same thing—dough made of flour, salt, baking powder, and water and fried in oil. The fried bread is the foundation of the popular Navajo/Indian tacos. According to Navajo tradition, "frybread" was created in the mid-1800s when they were forced on reservations and given rations of flour, salt, and lard by the government. They turned that into food and also ate it

when the Navajo living in Arizona were forced to make the 300-mile journey known as the "Long Walk" in 1864.

Western newspapers didn't start writing about the bread until 1930s and the tacos until the 1950s. This recipe is the signature dish of the lodge, and it's been a staple on their menu for many years. Zion's taco was created by their chef, Andrea Mendoza, who is from Arizona. Chef Andrea shared this about their chili recipe: "Chili ingredients are beef, crushed tomato and tomato sauce, pinto beans, a secret blend of spices, garlic, green chiles, onion, beef broth, and salt and pepper. We cook it over low simmering heat for hours to bring out the spices and flavor. Also made with love." This recipe is based on the list of ingredients provided by Chef Andrea and one that appeared in the *Arizona Republic* in 1954.

SERVES 6

2 cups flour

½ teaspoon salt

2½ teaspoons baking powder

¾ cup hot water or more

2 tablespoons vegetable oil

1 quart vegetable oil, for frying

Chili, cheddar cheese, lettuce, tomato, guacamole, and sour cream, for topping

1. Combine the flour, salt, and baking powder in a large mixing bowl and stir to blend. Gradually add the water and mix with a spoon until combined. It should be sticky.

2. Drizzle enough oil over the dough to keep it from drying out. Cover and let dough rest for 30 minutes.

3. The dough can be rolled out to ¼-inch thick and cut into 5 to 6 inch squares. Or it can be pinched and torn into small balls and patted thin.

4. Place enough oil in a pot so the depth is 2 inches and heat the oil to 350°F. Fry each piece until golden brown, flipping halfway through. Break any bubbles in the dough as it fries. Transfer to a paper towel–lined plate to drain.

5. Top with your favorite chili, cheddar cheese, lettuce, tomato, guacamole, and sour cream. Serve immediately.

DESSERTS

BOSTON CREAM PIE

1800s, PARKER HOUSE, BOSTON, MASSACHUSETTS

In 1865 the Parker House offered desserts that included cream pie, cream cakes, and Washington pie, of which some are versions of what is known today as Boston Cream Pie.

As early as the 1860s, Bostonians were enjoying a dessert called Boston Cream Cake, which was basically a cream puff made with a pâte à choux batter. But by 1872 a Boston cookbook called *The Dessert Book* by "A Boston Lady" included a recipe that was a sponge cake split in half and filled with vanilla custard, which she called a cream pie. Around the turn of the century, recipes for Boston Cream Pie were being published in the Boston papers that closely resembled the signature dish of the Parker House. Their recipe was so popular that in 1958 it became a Betty Crocker boxed mix. For more history on the Parker House, see the Parker House Rolls recipe.

MAKES 1 CAKE

1 (10-inch round) sponge cake (recipe follows)

Pastry cream (recipe follows)

Chocolate ganache (recipe follows)

White chocolate (recipe follows)

4 ounces toasted almonds, crushed

1. Level the sponge cake off at the top using a slicing knife. Cut the cake into two layers.

2. Spread the pastry cream over the bottom layer. Top with the second cake layer. Reserve a small amount of the pastry cream to spread on the sides of the cake.

3. Spread a thin layer of chocolate ganache on the top of the cake.

4. Follow immediately with spiral lines starting from the center of the cake, using the white chocolate in the pastry bag. Score the white lines with the point of a paring knife, starting at the center and pulling outward to the edge. The pattern should resemble a circular spider web.

5. Spread the sides of the cake with a thin coating of the reserved pastry cream. Press on the toasted almonds.

SPONGE CAKE

1 ounce butter

8 ounces sugar

7 eggs, beaten

1 cup cake flour

1 teaspoon baking powder

1 cup whole milk

1. In a bowl, combine the butter and sugar. Add a third of the eggs to the bowl and mix thoroughly.

2. Add the remaining eggs, cake flour, baking powder, and milk. Mix well.

3. Pour the mixture into a 10-inch greased cake pan. Bake at 350°F for about 20 minutes, or until spongy and golden.

4. Remove from the oven and allow to cool fully.

PASTRY CREAM

1 tablespoon butter

2 cups milk

2 cups heavy cream

½ cup sugar

1 teaspoon vanilla

3½ tablespoons cornstarch

6 eggs

1. Bring the butter, milk, heavy cream, half of the sugar, and vanilla to a boil in a saucepan.

2. While this mixture is cooking, combine the remaining sugar, cornstarch, and eggs in a bowl and whip until ribbons form.

3. When the milk, cream, and butter mixture reaches the boiling point, slowly whisk in the egg mixture and bring to a boil. Boil for approximately 1 minute.

4. Pour the pastry cream into a bowl and cover the surface with plastic wrap. Chill overnight if possible.

5. When chilled, whisk to smooth out the mixture.

CHOCOLATE GANACHE

1 cup heavy cream

16 ounces semi-sweet chocolate chunks

1. Bring the heavy cream just to a boil.

2. Pour the cream over the chocolate chunks and blend, then let it cool before spreading.

WHITE CHOCOLATE

1 ounce white chocolate "coins" or bars

1. Warm the white chocolate over boiling water to approximately 105°F.

2. Place in a piping bag with a ⅛-inch tip.

SISTER LIZZIE'S SHAKER SUGAR PIE

1803, GOLDEN LAMB, LEBANON, OHIO

The Golden Lamb began serving food and offering shelter to road-weary customers in 1803, which is the same year Ohio became a state. Since its beginnings it has been a gathering place for the community as well as travelers. For more history, see their Sauerkraut Balls recipe.

There is a bit of mystery as to where the Shaker Sugar Pie originated—some believe it was the Shaker community of West Union (near modern-day Churubusco, Indiana) in 1827. However, in 1805 Union Shaker Village, near Lebanon, Ohio, was formed, which dates back prior to the West Union community.

After Robert "Bob" and Virginia "Ginny" Jones purchased the Golden Lamb, money was tight. Being frugal, they purchased many of the furnishings at local yard sales and auctions.

At one auction Ginny purchased the antique Shaker hutch that sits in the hotel lobby today. She found a secret drawer in the hutch, which held a recipe titled "Sister Lizzie's Pie." Ginny had the chef make the recipe, which he tasted and loved. This happened around the 1928 holiday season and they put it on the menu. Guests loved the pie, and the rest is history!

MAKES 1 PIE

1¼ **cups sifted flour**

¼ **teaspoon salt**

½ **cup shortening, chilled**

2–3 **tablespoons cold water**

1 **cup brown sugar, packed firmly**

⅓ **cup flour**

2 **cups half-and-half**

Pinch of freshly grated nutmeg

1 **tablespoon butter**

Whipped cream, for garnish

1. To make the crust, whisk the 1¼ cups sifted flour and salt together in a medium-size bowl. With a pastry blender, cut in the cold shortening until the mixture resembles coarse crumbs.

2. Drizzle 2 tablespoons of ice water over the flour mixture. Toss with a fork to moisten, adding more water a few drops at a time until the dough comes together.

3. Gently gather the dough particles together into a ball. Wrap in plastic wrap and chill for at least 30 minutes before rolling.

4. Once chilled, roll out the dough and put it in a 9-inch pie plate.

5. Place the brown sugar, ⅓ cup flour, half-and-half, nutmeg, and butter into a medium saucepan and warm over low heat, stirring frequently.

6. Pour the warmed mixture into the uncooked piecrust. Place the pie on a half-sheet tray and bake in a 325°F oven for approximately 1 hour.

7. Remove the pie from the oven and allow it to rest for 30 minutes.

8. Garnish with whipped cream.

Chef Nick modified the recipe garnish by adding a caramelized sugar shell to the top of the pie. After the pie has cooled, dust the top of the pie with granulated sugar. Using a butane torch, gently heat the sugar until it first liquefies and then turns a rich caramel color, giving the pie an extra-special finish.

CHOCOLATE CHESS PIE

1960, ANGUS BARN, RALEIGH, NORTH CAROLINA

It was June 28, 1960, when the double doors of the red barn swung wide and owners Thad Eure Jr. and Charles Winston opened their restaurant. Neither had any restaurant experience, but their establishment is a testament to their incomparable hospitality, impeccable meals of quality, and the restaurant's rich, rustic Americana ambience.

According to the Angus Barn, "The original restaurant seated 275 and cost approximately $200,000 to build. Who would dare extend credit of that amount to two young dreamers whose dreams far exceeded their limited assets? Acquiring the necessary capital to pay for construction challenged the young hopefuls. Bank after bank declined Eure and Winston, politely referring to their venture as 'impossible' and 'a poor risk.' Borrowing from every person who had a modicum of faith in them, Eure and Winston raised money. Finally in desperation, Eure turned to his father, the late North Carolina Secretary of State Thad Eure, Sr., for the majority of the capital. In good faith, the senior Eure mortgaged his home to guarantee the loan, proclaiming, 'I believe in those boys!' Construction began immediately.

The Angus Barn owners and their wives, Alice and Flo, poured their energies and time into planning every detail of the restaurant. No task was too menial, no goal too daunting for the young couples. If experience is the best teacher, the young restaurateurs had much to learn. When the first Saturday night crowd in 1960 produced a mountain of dishes, the dishwashers walked off the job, leaving the young couples to clean dishes from late Saturday night through sunrise on Sunday. Later Eure recalled that although he appreciated his kitchen staff, he did not realize how much he valued their opinions until the dish washing disaster. Throughout their first week, using a three-compartment sink, the employees warned that it would be insufficient come Saturday night. Eure later remarked, 'That's when we learned our first big lesson: Listen to your staff and they will guide you wisely.'"

The Angus Barn's Chocolate Chess Pie is wildly popular and was developed by Alice Eure in the late 1960s. She had some help from kitchen manager Betty Shugart, who was a fifty-year employee of the restaurant. An estimated 50,000 Chocolate Chess Pies are made and sold each year!

MAKES 1 PIE

1 stick (½ cup) butter

4 ounces semi-sweet chocolate

1 cup sugar

2 eggs, beaten

1 teaspoon vanilla

Dash of salt

1 unbaked piecrust

1. Melt the butter and chocolate. Set aside.

2. Mix the sugar, eggs, vanilla, and salt together in a large bowl. Add the melted butter and chocolate and mix well.

3. Pour the mixture into the piecrust and bake for 35 minutes at 350°F.

4. Let cool before slicing and serve topped with whipped cream or vanilla ice cream.

PECAN PIE

1910, PARTRIDGE INN, AUGUSTA, GEORGIA

The Partridge Inn was originally a private home in the 1890s and was turned into a seasonal hotel in 1910 by Morris W. Partridge. It was expanded over the years and in 1929 became what it is today. The hotel gained prominence as a central gathering place for the winter elite from the Northeast, hosting golf legends, presidents, and legendary tea dances in its grand halls and ballrooms. The ground floor housed a post office, telegraph office, flower shop, bookstore, barbershop, and hairdressing parlor. In addition to the traditional dining room, the inn offered music and dancing in the grill room, originally called the Palm Room. Around 1941 the name changed to the Bamboo Room until about 1970. It was also at that time that the dining room was called the Pine Room.

Over the years, the hotel had a variety of chefs including C. E. Clifford in 1915 and John Billias from 1917 to 1918. Henry Nielson was the chef-steward in 1923 and previously worked for the O'Henry in Greensboro, North Carolina. In 1932 Emory Cook was a butcher and the chef at the inn. After hearing a story about former Louisiana governor Huey Long wanting pot likker on the menu, Emory said, "The United States Senate restaurant can't get ahead of the Partridge Inn. The first thing in the morning, pot likker will be on the main menu." In 1939 the inn announced that William Prescott was returning as the chef-steward for his eighth season. From 1946 to 1947 J. V. Dougherty, who was the chef at the Wardman Park Hotel, Washington, D.C., took over and specialized in Southern cooking. In 1957 the inn had its first female chef named Mamie Lou Dunn.

Georgia is known for its pecans, and the Partridge Inn prides itself on its pecan pie that they've been serving since at least 1926. The recipe has been tweaked by the chefs over the years, but it's a hotel staple. The current chef, Thomas Jacobs, loves to make everything from scratch and offers a seasonal menu using local ingredients. He also looks for healthier alternatives to classics, like this pecan pie recipe. It may be a "healthier" version, but it's still a decadent pie!

MAKES 1 PIE

3 cups flour

¼ cup sugar

1 teaspoon salt

10 ounces cold unsalted butter, cubed

2½ ounces cold shortening, cubed

½ cup ice water

1 cup light corn syrup

½ cup dark corn syrup

6 ounces soft cream cheese

1 cup packed brown sugar

3 ounces melted butter

6 large eggs, room temperature

2 teaspoons vanilla extract

1 teaspoon ground cinnamon

¾ teaspoon salt

3 cups toasted pecan halves

1. To make the crust, place the flour, sugar, and salt in the bowl of a food processor and pulse a few times to combine. Add the cold cubed butter and shortening and pulse in short bursts until it's cut into the dry ingredients and the mixture has the texture of coarse crumbs.

2. Add half of the ice water and pulse in 5-second bursts, adding the rest a little at a time until the dough just starts to come together. You may not need to use all of the water—stop when the dough starts to come together, and don't overwork it.

3. Turn the dough out onto a lightly floured surface and knead it just enough to incorporate any dry patches of flour. Shape it into a disc, wrap it well in plastic wrap, and refrigerate it for 1 hour to let it rest and chill.

4. After an hour, roll the dough out on a lightly floured surface until about ¼ inch thick. Lay it in a deep 11-inch pie pan and trim the excess from the sides. Prick the bottom of the crust with fork tines, then put it in the freezer to chill for 15 minutes while you preheat the oven to 350°F.

5. Once the oven's ready and the dough is chilled, spray a piece of foil with nonstick spray and press it, sprayed side down, on top of the pie dough. Fill the pie shell with beans or rice, then bake it for 20 minutes, until the sides of the crust look set and start taking on some color. Carefully remove the foil and beans and then continue to bake the crust for an additional 15 minutes, until it is no longer raw in the center and is starting to color.

6. To make the filling, whisk together the corn syrups, cream cheese, and brown sugar in a large bowl until smooth and free of lumps. Add the melted butter and then the eggs one at a time. Finally, add the vanilla extract, cinnamon, and salt and whisk until smooth.

7. Put the pecans in the cooled piecrust and then pour the filling mixture on top. Tap the pie pan against the counter several times to pop any air bubbles.

8. Place the pie on a baking sheet covered with parchment paper to keep your oven from getting messy in the event of any spills.

9. Bake the pie for 20 minutes at 375°F, then turn the oven down to 350°F and bake for an additional 55 to 65 minutes, until the pie is puffed, there are a few cracks along the sides, and the center doesn't jiggle like gelatin when the pie is tapped. If the outer edges of the crust appear to be getting too dark during the baking process, cover the edges loosely with foil strips.

10. Once baked, remove the pie from the oven and cool to room temperature. It's wonderful but messy when eaten warm, and it's also delicious at room temperature or even chilled.

11. Serve with whipped cream or ice cream, and refrigerate leftovers for up to a week.

If you'd like, you can roll out the excess dough and cut small shapes out of it, like ovals or leafs. Once the crust is baked and cooled, brush the rim with beaten egg and place the crust cutouts around the edge. Brush the top of the cutouts with more beaten egg and sprinkle it with a little sugar. Fill the crust and bake as described above. This method of decoration takes a little more time, but it looks wonderful and it prevents the edges of the crust from getting overdone since the edges are baked along with the filling and are not pre-baked like the rest of the crust.

CHOCOLATE PECAN PIE

1929, MILLER'S, RONKS, PENNSYLVANIA

This Amish pie recipe has been served at Miller's since the early days and is still a popular menu item. For a detailed history of Miller's, see the Chicken and Waffles recipe.

MAKES 1 PIE

3 eggs

1¼ cups sugar

¼ teaspoon salt

1½ teaspoons vanilla

1¼ teaspoons milk powder

2½ tablespoons flour

1 tablespoon butter

1½ tablespoons shortening

1¼ cups light corn syrup

1¼ cups pecan pieces

¼ cup chocolate chips

1 (10-inch) unbaked piecrust

1. Beat the eggs with the sugar, salt, and vanilla in a large bowl.

2. In a small bowl, combine the milk powder and flour. Add to the egg mixture and beat for 3 minutes.

3. Melt the butter and shortening in a saucepan and cook over medium heat until lightly browned. Stir in the corn syrup. Add the melted fats and corn syrup to the mixture and beat for another 2 minutes.

4. Add the pecan pieces and chocolate chips and mix by hand to blend.

5. Pour the filling into the piecrust and bake at 400°F for 10 minutes. Reduce the heat to 375°F and bake for an additional 25 minutes or until firm on top.

SHENANDOAH APPLE PIE

1931, THE MIMSLYN INN, LURAY, VIRGINIA

Henry and Elizabeth Mims opened the Mimslyn Inn in the Shenandoah Valley in May 1931. Together with Henry's brothers, the couple began constructing the hotel upon a piece of land that once belonged to a historic estate known as Aventine Hall. The family imported all kinds of upscale building materials from across the commonwealth, from high-end stone to durable wood. The construction took fifteen months. When visitors and guests entered the Mimslyn, they saw an amazing array of distinctive architectural details and lavish amenities. An eye-catching feature was an impressive winding staircase that one of Henry's brothers, J. R., designed himself. To celebrate the opening, the Mimses held a massive soiree that was attended by several hundred people. The Mims family graciously welcomed guests into their new home for many years thereafter.

Apple pie is an American staple, but this signature recipe was created here. Apple pie has been a signature dish at the Mimslyn because a key ingredient of the recipe is grown on the inn's property. Residents of the area remember when the inn baked fresh apple pies for

the resorts along Skyline Drive. The apples of the Shenandoah Valley have a distinctive tart flavor that sets them apart from other pie apples. It is known that Johnny Appleseed was a notable resident of the Shenandoah Valley. Chef Chris Harris has been with the Mimslyn for thirteen years and hasn't changed this historic pie recipe, but he did add a twist by serving it with his signature Vanilla Bourbon Ice Cream.

MAKES 1 PIE

2 unbaked piecrusts

3 cups thickly sliced apples

1 cup grated cheese (cheddar works well)

1 cup sugar

1 tablespoon flour

1 tablespoon melted butter

½ teaspoon grated nutmeg

½ teaspoon cinnamon

1. Line a 9-inch pie plate with the first crust.

2. Place all of the ingredients, except the second piecrust, in a bowl and mix to combine. Pour the filling into the piecrust and top with the second crust.

3. Bake at 350°F for about 45 minutes, until the apples are soft.

4. Serve with Vanilla Bourbon Ice Cream (recipe on page 217).

COCONUT CREAM PIE

1944, THE WILLOWS, HONOLULU, HAWAII

The Willows' world-famous, mile-high coconut cream pie is something they've been making since its opening. Food columnist and *Los Angeles Times* reporter Clementine Paddelford wrote a story in *This Week Magazine* called "Why The Willows?" in 1964. She reported, "It tastes, smells, feels like Hawaii should. Another reason to go is to feed the 20-lb carp in the garden pool. Give your calories to the carp. Then make it go up when you order dessert. The truth is, I go to eat that coconut cream pie. Mrs. Carol Ellerbrake, the chef, bakes the pies which, topped with meringue, stand four inches tall. There are many reasons for going to The Willows. You go, of course, to eat the curry with the tag-alongs in the six-sectioned monkeypod dish designed as a mango leaf. But what everyone goes to eat, and comes back for again, is this coconut cream pie." The pie was so good that *Family Circle* magazine featured the Willows and their pie in their January 1969 issue. See the Chicken Kama'aina recipe for additional history on the Willows.

Mrs. Carol Ellerbrake, chef at The Willows, displays one of her famous confections.

MAKES 1 PIE

2 cups milk

½ plus ¼ cup sugar, divided

Pinch of salt

¼ cup freshly grated coconut

2 heaping tablespoons cornstarch

4 eggs, separated

1 tablespoon butter

Vanilla, to taste

1 pre-baked piecrust

Grated coconut for topping

1. Place the milk, ½ cup sugar, salt, and grated coconut in a saucepan and bring to a near boil.

2. Mix the cornstarch and the egg yolks with a little water to moisten the cornstarch and then add to the saucepan. Cook over low heat, stirring continuously, until thick.

3. Remove the saucepan from the heat and add the butter and vanilla. Stir to blend.

4. Allow the filling to cool and then add to the pre-baked piecrust.

5. To make the meringue, beat the egg whites until stiff peaks form. Gradually add ¼ cup sugar and beat until shiny.

6. Cover the pie filling with the meringue and sprinkle with coconut.

7. Bake in a 400°F oven until the meringue is golden brown. Chill before serving.

APPLE CRISP

1886, BASIN HARBOR, VERGENNES, VERMONT

Local teacher Ardelia Beach lived in Vermont and was engaged to be married, with her future seemingly planned out for her. However, after her fiancé died in the Civil War, she went west to Iowa, where she taught school. She returned to Vermont when her brothers told her the Basin Harbor farm was for sale. In 1882 she became the new owner, put out lawn chairs so guests could enjoy Lake Champlain, and turned it into a resort. Adelia's idea stayed in the family after she died in 1909, and the resort has been run by various members of the Beach family to this day.

The first mention of apple crisp didn't show up in newspapers until the 1890s, so it's possible that Ardelia Beach invented it. There's neither proof for nor against her, but she created her recipe back in 1886. Her recipe has been a staple on the menu since then and it's served a la mode. It was her tradition to make it for every holiday, and Basin Harbor guests can still enjoy it today in the Red Mill Restaurant or the main dining room of the resort, which was renamed Ardelia's to honor her memory. This dish uses locally sourced ingredients including McIntosh apples from various orchards around Vermont as well as apples grown on trees found on the resort property itself.

Ardelia's granddaughter, Pennie Beach, shared this fond memory: "Nothing says Autumn like Grandma Beach's Apple Crisp! There was a group of old apple trees near our house

when I was growing up, which contained a variety of different types of fruit. Apples for pies and cakes, and others for cider or just plain eating, most with long-forgotten names, except for the all-important McIntosh, the king of apples for apple crisp. My brother, Bob, and I loved to take a basket from our kitchen to gather the fruit, a treat of tart sweetness. We would watch our mom carefully prepare the dish, knowing that it would generate wonderful smells as it cooked. After all the years, it continues to be our favorite dessert."

SERVES 6–8

10–12 apples, McIntosh or Granny Smith

¼ cup dark brown sugar

¼ cup white sugar

¼ cup all-purpose flour

Cinnamon and/or nutmeg to taste (the original recipe did not contain either)

1 stick (½ cup) butter, frozen

1. Peel, core, and thinly slice the apples, then pile them into a greased baking dish.

2. Combine the sugars, flour, and cinnamon and/or nutmeg in a bowl. Spread over the apples, then grate the butter evenly over the top. If the apples seem dry, add ¼ cup water to the bottom of the dish, taking care to not get the topping wet.

3. Bake at 350°F for 45 minutes. Let cool for at least 30 minutes before serving.

4. Top with vanilla ice cream, whipped cream, crème fraîche, or plain Greek yogurt if you like.

BLUEBERRY TORTE

1912, HOMEWOOD INN, YARMOUTH, MAINE

Before the Homewood Inn came to be, a seafaring captain named James Munroe Bucknam built a home on Casco Bay on 115 acres in 1742. Fast-forward to 1912, when Burton Prentiss Lyman bought the property and turned it into the Homewood at Yarmouth-by-the-Sea. After Lyman passed away in 1942, it was purchased by Fred and Doris Webster in 1947 and became the Homewood Inn.

In 1958 the Websters bought the Wescustogo Inn located at the junction of Highway 88 and Pleasant Street to use as an annex for the Homewood's overflow. In the 1950s Bette Davis stayed at the inn for six months, and she mentioned her stay in her autobiography. She wrote, "When I was well enough, we said good-bye to New York, loaded the station wagon, Gary and I, a governess and the three children—plus Tinker Belle, B.D.'s poodle and a parakeet in a cage—and drove to Homewood Inn in Yarmouth, Maine, which Gary had found for us. We arrived there in April and stayed until September. The property is a few hundred feet from the shores of Casco Bay, which was a big draw for its guests."

By the 1960s Fred and Doris had turned the business over to their son, Fred Jr., and his wife, Colleen. The inn closed in 1992 but their history lives on through this recipe.

SERVES 8–10

4 eggs

1 cup sugar

1 teaspoon vanilla

½ cup water

1½ cups sifted flour

1½ teaspoons baking powder

⅛ teaspoon salt

2 cups blueberries

1 pint whipping cream

¼ cup powdered sugar

¼ cup sherry or Drambuie or 1 teaspoon vanilla

1. Beat the eggs in a large bowl until lemon-colored, about 10 minutes. Gradually stir in the sugar.

2. Combine the vanilla and water in a small bowl. Add to the egg-sugar mixture and blend well.

3. Sift the flour with the baking powder and salt. Add to the batter and stir to combine.

4. Divide the batter among six 9-inch cake pans that have been greased and lined with wax or parchment paper. Sprinkle the blueberries over the batter in all of the pans.

5. Bake at 375°F for about 12 to 15 minutes. Cool in the pans for 10 minutes and then remove and allow to cool completely on cakes racks.

6. To make the filling, whip the cream until thick and then add the powdered sugar and beat again. Add the liquor or vanilla and whip until stiff peaks form.

7. Place one of the cake layers, blueberry side up, onto a cake platter. Spread some of the whipped cream on top and repeat the process until you have used all the layers. The top layer should also have cream and is then dusted with powdered sugar.

8. Chill before serving.

Owner Doris Webster awaiting guests in front of one of her birch-laden fireplaces in the main house, 1963.

BROWNIE

1893, PALMER HOUSE, A HILTON HOTEL, CHICAGO, ILLINOIS

Potter Palmer was a Chicago business magnate who was well-known for a variety of endeavors, including his significant role in the development of downtown Chicago's iconic State Street. Palmer's former business partner, Marshall Field, introduced him to a wealthy socialite named Bertha Honoré, who was twenty-three years younger than him. That meeting led to an engagement, and the Palmer House would soon become the couple's contribution to Chicago. Sadly, the Palmer House fell victim to the Great Chicago Fire, just thirteen days after its grand opening. Potter was determined to rebuild his hotel and secured a $1.7 million loan. On November 8, 1873, the new Palmer House welcomed its first guests and served some of the city's best meals. In 1933 the hotel's Empire Dining Room was converted into an entertainment epicenter and supper club.

Now, on to the brownie. The original brownie was created in the Palmer House kitchen in the late nineteenth century at the direction of Bertha Palmer. She wanted to debut it at the 1893 Columbian Exposition World's Fair. This recipe is well over a century old, and it is the exact same one used for the brownie served in the Palmer House Hilton today.

9½ ounces 60% dark couverture chocolate

17½ ounces butter

23 ounces granulated sugar

6 ounces flour

1 teaspoon baking powder

8 eggs

12 ounces chopped walnuts

Brownie glaze

1. Melt the chocolate with the butter in a double boiler.

2. Combine the sugar, flour, and baking powder in a mixing bowl. Mix the chocolate into the dry ingredients, beating for 4 to 5 minutes. Add the eggs and blend to combine.

3. Pour the batter into a 9 x 13-inch baking tray. Sprinkle the walnuts on top and press the nuts down slightly into the mixture.

4. Bake in a 350°F oven for 35 minutes. You will know when it's done, as the edges will start to become a little crispy and the brownie will raise about ¼ inch. (Note: Even when the brownie is properly baked, it will test "gooey" with a toothpick in the middle due to the richness of the mixture.)

5. After removing from the oven, allow to cool about 30 minutes before spreading a thin layer of the glaze on top with a pastry brush.

BROWNIE GLAZE

1 cup water

1 cup apricot preserves

1 teaspoon unflavored gelatin

Add the water, preserves, and gelatin to a saucepan and mix thoroughly. Bring to a boil for 2 minutes. Use hot.

The brownies are easier to cut if you place the tray in the freezer for about 3 to 4 hours after glazing.

BANANAS FOSTER

1946, BRENNAN'S, NEW ORLEANS, LOUISIANA

Brennan's Vieux Carre Restaurant on Bourbon Street was started when Owen Brennan, who owned the Old Absinthe House, was teased by Count Arnaud. Arnaud told him that an Irishman's culinary skills ended with boiled potatoes, so Brennan wanted to prove him wrong. He opened his restaurant in 1946 and did just that. After a successful decade of business and Owen's untimely passing, the restaurant moved to its present site and is now owned by his nephew, Ralph Brennan. In true New Orleans style, Brennan's loyal patrons ate and drank a final supper before parading to dinner at the new location at 417 Royal Street.

Now, let's get to the famous Bananas Foster story. Did you know that bananas were not introduced to North America until sometime after the Civil War? It was a few decades later when they became popular and New Orleans became a major center for banana imports from Central and South America. According to Brennan's, by 1899 Sicilian immigrants Joseph, Luca, and Felix Vaccaro, together with Salvador D'Antoni, were importing bananas from La Ceiba, Honduras, for their produce cart in the French Market. This produce cart was the forerunner of the Standard Fruit Company, which was established in 1924 by the Vaccaro brothers.

Ralph Brennan's great-grandparents were Mr. and Mrs. Joseph Vaccaro of the family that started the Standard Fruit Company. Brennan's noted that "Ralph has fond memories of his mother telling him about her travels as a teenager to distant lands on the family's banana steamships." Standard's competitor, United Fruit Company, was also established in 1899 and those two companies were primarily responsible for bringing bananas into the ports of New Orleans for American consumption. And while these companies were competitors, they also helped each other get bananas into New Orleans, as Standard had steamships while United owned a large portion of the railroads that helped transport bananas. By 1915 Standard's business had grown so large that it bought most of the ice factories in New Orleans in order to refrigerate its banana shipments, leading to its president at the time, Joseph Vaccaro, becoming known as the "Ice King."

In the early 1950s, Owen Brennan decided to name a dessert after his friend and fellow member of the Metropolitan Crime Commission, Richard Foster. At the time, Owen's younger brother and Ralph's father, John, was running Brennan's Processed Potato Company. They had a surplus of bananas, so Owen asked his sister Ella and Chef Paul Blangé to come up with a new dessert using bananas. Ella recalled her mother, Nell Valentine-Brennan, brûléeing bananas for breakfast. It was that memory and creativity that led to the invention of Bananas Foster at Brennan's Vieux Carré Restaurant on Bourbon Street, across from the Old Absinthe House.

SERVES 2

1 ounce butter

½ cup light brown sugar

¼ teaspoon cinnamon

1½ ounces banana liqueur

1 banana, peeled and cut lengthwise

1½ ounces aged rum

Vanilla ice cream

1. Combine the butter, sugar, and cinnamon in a flambé pan. As the butter melts under medium heat, add the banana liqueur and stir to combine.

2. As the sauce starts to cook, add the banana to the pan. Cook the banana halves until they begin to soften, about 1 to 2 minutes.

3. Tilt the pan back to slightly heat the far edge. Once hot, carefully add the rum and tilt the pan toward the flame to ignite it. Stir the sauce to ensure that all of the alcohol cooks out.

4. Place one banana half into each serving dish. Serve with ice cream and top with the sauce in the pan.

BOCAROONS

According to legend and the Boca Raton Inn, famed American architect and founder of the inn, Addison Mizner, possessed one of history's greatest sweet tooths. Mizner wore silk pajamas and often traveled down to the bake shop of the hotel in the middle of the night with his three pet monkeys and possibly a parrot to wake up his pastry chef. The late-night excursions often found Mizner and his pets eating warm, out-of-the-oven, orange-scented coconut and chocolate cookies.

Mizner considered the *Bocaroon*, as it affectionately became known, to be the perfect treat for him and his feathered and furry friends. According to the inn, "A little coconut for the parrot, orange for the monkeys, and a touch of chocolate for himself—just enough cookie to last them through the night. Always the visionary, Addison Mizner was ahead of his time with the local farm-to-table concept. Together with Mizner, the pastry chef prepared the sweet treats with local Florida citrus, orange, and coconuts. Florida sugar cane had started to be planted on the west coast and Cubans started to migrate and farm the sugar-bearing stalks. The rest is sweet history as the recipe has stood the test of time and is still served today. A macaroon is very different from classical French (very popular) Macarons; macaroons are a small cake or biscuit, or drop cookie typically made from shaved coconut and sugar."

MAKES 45 BOCAROONS

Zest from ¼ orange

1 teaspoon coconut extract

1 teaspoon vanilla extract

1 cup shredded coconut

⅔ cup egg whites (3 eggs)

½ cup plus 6 tablespoons sugar, divided

¼ cup corn syrup

¼ cup shortening

1. Combine the orange zest, coconut extract, vanilla extract, shredded coconut, egg whites, and ½ cup sugar.

2. In a double boiler, combine the corn syrup, shortening, and 6 tablespoons sugar. Heat until the shortening melts.

3. Once the shortening melts, pour into the shredded coconut mix and combine all the ingredients.

4. Pipe Bocaroons onto a sheet tray and bake in a 335°F oven for about 16 minutes or until golden brown.

BUTTERSCOTCH COOKIES

1930s, GRAYLYN ESTATE,
WINSTON-SALEM, NORTH CAROLINA

Graylyn Estate was one of the last of the sprawling family mansions to be built in America, and it was only second in size to Biltmore Estate in Asheville, North Carolina. Bowman Gray was the chairman of R.J. Reynolds and had become enormously successful by 1927, when he and his wife Nathalie began construction of their home in Winston-Salem. They moved into the 46,000-square-foot home in 1932 and Nathalie began entertaining. The Grays were a welcoming and charitable couple who donated to the community, so it' not surprising that Mrs. Gray welcomed her guests with open arms and a sweet treat.

The story goes, as recalled by the longtime poulterer and close family friend of the Grays, Louie Baker, the cookies were named after the family's beloved Scottish terriers, Butter and Scotch. The cookies are still served daily to Graylyn Estate guests to honor Mrs. Gray.

MAKES ABOUT 2 DOZEN COOKIES

1 pound butter, softened

8 ounces brown sugar

8 ounces white sugar

3 eggs

1 teaspoon vanilla extract

1 pound flour

1 teaspoon baking soda

Pinch of salt

¼ cup butterscotch morsels

1. Cream the butter and sugars together. Add the eggs and vanilla extract.

2. Mix the flour, baking soda, salt, and butterscotch morsels into the butter-sugar mixture until the dough is smooth.

3. Portion the dough into 2- to 3.5-ounce balls. Place onto a greased baking sheet and bake at 375°F for 10 to 12 minutes.

4. Allow to cool to room temperature.

WHITE CHOCOLATE CHIP COOKIES

1965, WHITE STALLION RANCH, TUCSON, ARIZONA

These cookies have been served at White Stallion Ranch since the True family took over and hired chef Judy Bellini. She was the first employee hired by Allen True when he bought the ranch in 1965. She was seventeen years old at the time and is still serving up dishes at the ranch today! Third-generation Steven True said, "She babysat my father, my uncle, and me and my brother, too! She married here and her husband was also an employee until he retired (he has since passed), and her kids were raised here." For more history on the ranch, see the Breakfast Ride Potatoes recipe.

MAKES 2 DOZEN COOKIES

1 cup shortening

1 cup white sugar

1 cup brown sugar

2 eggs

1 teaspoon vanilla

2 cups coarsely crushed potato chips

1 (6-ounce) package white chocolate chips

2½ cups flour

1 teaspoon baking soda

1. Cream the shortening and sugars together in a large bowl until light and fluffy.

2. Add the eggs and vanilla and beat well.

3. Add the crushed potato chips and white chocolate chips and stir to blend.

4. Sift the flour and baking soda into a small bowl and then stir into the creamed mixture.

5. Drop dough onto a greased cookie sheet and bake at 375°F for 10 to 12 minutes.

SEA SALT CHOCOLATE CHIP COOKIES

1816, INN AT PERRY CABIN, ST. MICHAELS, MARYLAND

Chef Gregory James feels that all guests at the Inn at Perry Cabin should be made to feel special and welcomed. Part of his contribution are distinct menu items for the guests and a different house-made specialty cookie at turndown every night. These are his chocolate chip cookies that are topped with an Eastern Shore sea salt called Barrier Islands Salt. For the history of the inn, see the Crab Imperial Scotch Egg recipe.

3½ cups butter

2¾ cups granulated sugar

1 pound plus 12 ounces dark brown sugar

2¾ pounds flour

¾ teaspoon sea salt

2 teaspoons baking soda

3 cups Callebaut bittersweet chocolate chips

4 whole eggs

4 egg yolks

1 ounce vanilla extract

Barrier Islands Salt, for topping

1. Melt the butter over medium heat and allow it to cook until it begins to lightly brown and smell like caramel. Remove from the stove and refrigerate until solid. Once the refrigerated butter is solid, cut it into ⅜-inch cubes.

2. In the bowl of a standing mixer, add the sugars and mix until they are thoroughly combined.

3. Add the cut-up butter, flour, salt, baking soda, and chocolate chips and mix until fully incorporated.

4. Add the whole eggs, egg yolks, and vanilla, keeping the mixer on low speed until all ingredients look crumbled. Pull out a little and see if you can ball it in your hand. If it stays together, it's done. If it's too crumbly, continue to mix a little longer.

5. Transfer the dough to a clean, dry bowl and place in the refrigerator to chill the butter back up. (For best results the butter needs to be as cold as possible before baking.)

6. On a parchment-lined sheet pan, with a tablespoon measure, portion out 35 cookies into well-spaced rows of 5 by 7. With gloved fingers, lightly press the top of each cookie to create a dimple.

7. Add ¼ teaspoon of Barrier Island Sea Salt to the top of each cookie.

8. Bake at 350°F for about 4 minutes, turn the pan, and bake for another 4 minutes. Set on a rack to cool for service.

ALMOND MACAROONS

1913, HOTEL DU PONT, WILMINGTON, DELAWARE

The twelve-story Italian Renaissance building housing the Hotel Du Pont debuted in 1913 after a two-and-a-half-year construction process that was a true labor of love. French and Italian craftsmen carved, gilded, and painted this extraordinarily detailed architectural gem. After opening, the hotel instantly gained international fame, rivaling the finest hotels in New York and Europe while serving as the financial and social epicenter for the Wilmington elite. Expansion of the property in 1918 brought the additions of the Du Barry Room, the Gold Ballroom, and the theater, now known as the Playhouse on Rodney Square.

In 1927 the Du Pont hired pastry chef William Hartmann, who was born in Berne, Switzerland, in 1900. He was the second eldest of the six boys and three girls of Emil Hartmann and apprenticed in pastry baking in Berne and Leysia in Switzerland. In order to do that, he worked fourteen- and fifteen-hour days for three years and only received room and board.

He also learned to speak German and English. Upon his arrival in New York City, Hartmann went to work at the Commodore as the assistant pastry chef for the Bowman-Biltmore chain, which also owned the Hotel Du Pont–Biltmore. He married Louise Askent of Manheim, Germany, in 1925 and they moved to Wilmington in 1927 when he was hired as head pastry chef for the Hotel Du Pont.

Hartmann quickly gained a reputation for his pastry skills and his unique holiday treats. At Christmas he created a ship completely made of nougat, and for Easter he made groups of both large and small chocolate eggs with flowers in a variety of pastel shades. He told a newspaper that he used about 400 pounds of flour, 100 pounds of sugar, sixty quarts of cream, and forty dozen eggs daily to provide pastry and bread for the guests. He also noted they made about forty gallons of ice cream each day. He stayed at the hotel until 1947, when he opened the Brandywine Pastry Shop.

It's almost a given that Hartmann is responsible for creating the hotel's signature almond macaroons, since they've been baked there since 1940. The cookies are served with all lunches, dinners, and banquet events in this historic hotel. These delicious macaroons are so popular that the bake shop makes more than 400,000 per month. Gluten-free and containing only four ingredients, the recipe is simple yet truly unique to the Hotel Du Pont. These macaroons are served in the hotel's signature restaurant, the Green Room, known for opulent design elements that bring the elegance and grandeur of the Gilded Age into the twenty-first century.

MAKES ABOUT 5 DOZEN MACAROONS

1 cup plus 2 tablespoons sugar

21 ounces almond paste

5 large egg whites, lightly beaten

½ teaspoon vanilla

1. Beat together the sugar and almond paste until the mixture is smooth.

2. Beat in the egg whites and vanilla until the mixture is combined.

3. Transfer the mixture to a pastry bag that has been fitted with a ½-inch plain round tip.

4. Line a baking sheet with wax paper and pipe ¾-inch-wide mounds 1½ inches apart. Let stand for 2 hours.

5. Bake in a 400°F oven for 8 to 10 minutes or until pale golden brown.

6. Lift the wax paper gently and pour 3 tablespoons of water between the baking sheet and wax paper, and let the cookies steam loose for 15 seconds.

7. Transfer to a rack and let cool completely.

If your oven heats from the bottom, stack two cookie sheets together before lining and piping so the cookies won't scorch.

PECAN BALL

1887, GRAND HOTEL, MACKINAC ISLAND, MICHIGAN

Mackinac Island became a summer getaway for people in the Midwest after the Civil War, but accommodations were limited. That all changed in 1887, however, when the Grand Hotel made its debut.

The Grand Pecan Ball is the Grand Hotel's signature dessert and has been served since 1948. The recipe was adapted from the L. S. Ayres department store that opened in Indianapolis in 1872. There was a tearoom in the store, and the pecan ball was a memorable dessert. The owners of the Grand Hotel enjoyed it so much that in 1948 they hired someone to re-create it to be served at the hotel. It very quickly became the resort's most popular dessert and is still loved by guests today. The hotel prepares over 60,000 Grand Pecan Balls every year. Ayres may be closed, but you can still enjoy their creation at the Grand, which created a special fudge sauce for the ball that's prepared on a daily basis from local ingredients.

2 cups chopped pecans

Fudge sauce

1 large scoop vanilla ice cream

1. Put the chopped pecans in a bowl. Pour as much fudge as you'd like into a chilled single-serving dish.

2. Roll the scoop of ice cream in the pecans, making sure it is fully coated.

3. Set the pecan ball on top of the fudge sauce.

FUDGE SAUCE
SERVES 6

¼ cup plus 1 tablespoon butter

1¾ cups powdered sugar

¼ cup Trimoline invert sugar syrup

¾ cup plus 1 tablespoon plus ¾ teaspoon evaporated milk

½ cup plus 1 tablespoon chocolate chips

1. Melt the butter, sugar, and Trimoline in a saucepan over low heat, stirring frequently.

2. Whisk in the evaporated milk.

3. Add the chocolate chips and whisk until blended and smooth.

GOLD BRICK SUNDAE
1928, SEA ISLAND RESORT, SEA ISLAND, GEORGIA

A. W. "Bill" Jones and automobile magnate Howard Coffin opened the Cloister in October 1928 on a foundation of genuine warmth and hospitality, creating "a friendly little hotel" on the southern coast of Georgia. Due to the ingenuity of Jones during the Depression, the Sea Island Company issued its own scrip (scrip was issued by a company to pay its employees, and it could only be exchanged in company stores owned by the employer) to employees, and every business in the county honored it.

The chef de cuisine was Tony Marchetty, and his kitchen was a modern marvel at the time. It was white with gas and electric stoves, electric dishwashers, steam-heated warming ovens, and plate and platter warmers with racks. It also contained automatic toasters, electric egg cookers, electric refrigerators, a bread mixer, and a mayonnaise mixer. The chefs made a myriad of dishes and used the local bounty of the ocean to include seafood on every menu. Favorite dishes included Baked Oysters Cloisters, Cream of Crab Soup Guale, and Terrapin a la Sea Island.

Around 1942 Elmer's Chocolate of New Orleans started bottling their Gold Brick Sundae topping. It became a hit around the country, and restaurants and hotels made the sundae their signature dish. The Cloisters did the same and is still serving it today!

SERVES 4

4 ounces pecan pieces, roughly chopped

10 ounces milk chocolate, chopped

10 ounces dark chocolate, chopped

4½ sticks unsalted butter, melted

32 ounces vanilla ice cream

Whipped cream and 4 maraschino cherries, for garnish

1. Arrange the pecan pieces on a baking pan lined with parchment paper. Toast in a 325°F oven for about 10 minutes until fragrant and dark, stirring occasionally.

2. In a double boiler, melt the chopped milk chocolate and dark chocolate together. Whisk in the melted butter and remove from heat. Gently fold in the toasted pecans.

3. When ready to serve, place two 4-ounce scoops of ice cream in a chilled ice cream dish.

4. Gently warm the chocolate mixture until it can be poured over the ice cream. Garnish with a dollop of whipped cream and top with a maraschino cherry.

THOMAS JEFFERSON'S VANILLA ICE CREAM

1930, PRIDE DAIRY, BOTTINEAU, NORTH DAKOTA

Pride Dairy has been serving their signature vanilla ice cream and butter since 1930, when they started accepting surplus cream from local farmers. Even after making ice cream, they still had a surplus, so they turned it into butter that could easily be shipped by train to Minneapolis. They soon opened the Dairy Dipper, an ice cream parlor and lunch counter, to offer their products.

Pride, as well as a few other dairies, was approached by Xanterra Travel Collection in 2015 to see if they would be interested in re-creating Thomas Jefferson's original vanilla ice cream. Jefferson was known for making this and served it to dignitaries while he was the president of the United States. The goal was to serve Jefferson's original ice cream at Mount Rushmore in South Dakota so that visitors could taste this historic treat. Pride Dairy came up with the best interpretation and now makes the TJ Ice Cream. You can make Jefferson's ice cream in your own kitchen with this recipe, or sample it at Mount Rushmore or at various restaurants in North Dakota.

MAKES 1 QUART

6 egg yolks

1 cup sugar

Pinch of salt

4 cups heavy cream

2 teaspoons vanilla or 1 vanilla stick, split down the middle

1. Beat the egg yolks in a large saucepan until thick and lemon-colored. Gradually add the sugar and salt.

2. Pour the cream into a smaller saucepan and bring to a boil. If using a vanilla bean, add now.

3. Slowly add the cream to the egg mixture and cook over low heat, stirring constantly until thickened.

4. Strain through a fine sieve into a bowl and when cool add the vanilla if using extract.

5. Freeze according to ice cream machine instructions.

Thomas Jefferson's handwritten vanilla ice cream recipe, circa 1800s.

VANILLA BOURBON
ICE CREAM

1931, THE MIMSLYN INN, LURAY, VIRGINIA

This recipe was created by Chef Chris Harris to accompany the historic apple pie that's been served at the Mimslyn Inn for decades. This is his signature recipe that takes the pie to a whole new level! See the Shenandoah Apple Pie entry for a history of the inn.

ILene Meadows, Mozell Jewel, Elsie Wimer, Pearl Goode, Barbara and Haywood Taylor

MAKES 1½ QUARTS

3 cups half-and-half

1 cup heavy cream

2 vanilla beans

8 egg yolks

9 ounces sugar

¼ cup bourbon

1. Combine the half-and-half and cream in a saucepan.

2. Split the vanilla beans and scrape out the seeds. Add to the cream mixture.

3. Heat over low heat to scald the cream (look for bubbles around the edge of the pan).

4. In a separate bowl, beat the egg yolks and sugar until smooth.

5. Add a small amount of the cream mixture to the egg mixture, whipping constantly, to temper the mixture. Gradually add the remaining egg mixture to the pan and stir to blend.

6. Return to heat and stir until it reaches 160°F.

7. Strain into a bowl and then place in an ice cream machine. Turn in the machine until frozen.

8. Add the bourbon at the end and turn for another 10 minutes to incorporate it.

MANGO ICE CREAM

1859, MENGER HOTEL, SAN ANTONIO, TEXAS

The Menger Hotel was constructed in 1859 under the direction of owner William A. Menger and architect John Fries near Menger's brewery. The original two-story building offered fifty guest rooms and was constructed on Alamo Plaza. On January 18, 1859, the *San Antonio Herald* reported, "The Menger Hotel is rapidly drawing towards completion. The main room on the second floor is unsurpassed for beauty. The finishing of the walls and ceilings being developed and executed by our fellow citizen P.C. Taylor. The walls and ceilings unite the smoothness of glass to the whiteness of alabaster, whilst the mouldings are conceived in fine taste and executed in the best style of art."

After Menger died at the age of forty-four years in 1871, his wife Mary and son Louis William continued to operate the brewery and the hotel. The hotel became popular due to her meals that featured the best beef, chicken, and fresh country butter and eggs the markets had to offer. Mary created the menu selections that included everything from soup to nuts. In 1881 a third story was added to the hotel and then in 1887 a fourth story was added. It was in the Menger Bar that Theodore Roosevelt recruited his Volunteer Rough Riders who fought in Cuba during the Spanish-American War.

The Menger's Colonial Room Restaurant has been in operation since the hotel opened. Many of the restaurant's chefs came from Europe to create dishes reflecting the German, Mexican, French, and American blend of cultures found in San Antonio. By the late 1860s the hotel had firmly established its culinary reputation. Known for its wild game, the menu featured such exotic dishes as

wild turkey stuffed with chestnuts, spotted antelope, and dried buffalo tongue. Soup made from soft-shell turtles caught from the nearby San Antonio River was one of the dining room specialties. Many elaborate balls and cotillions, hosted by San Antonio's social and political elite, were held in this room. Often Spanish moss and other atmospheric flora were hung from the columns to create elaborate themes. Among the many celebrities who have dined here are Presidents Grant and McKinley, General Robert E. Lee, and French actress Sarah Bernhardt.

In 1912 the original restaurant was remodeled by noted San Antonio architect Atlee B. Ayres to reflect the prevailing neoclassical Greek and Roman style of that era. As part of the remodeling, the original cast-iron columns were enclosed with a Greek Revival style and carved wooden dentils, and arched window openings and other decorative millwork and mirrors were installed. The unusual plaster mantelpiece around the fireplace features two caryatids (a stone carving of a draped female figure, used as a pillar to support the entablature of a Greek or Greek-style building).

More than 130 years of refinements have created a masterpiece of traditional elegance and atmosphere. The Menger Hotel honors Mary Menger's cuisine and still offers her bread pudding and mango ice cream. The hotel's signature ice cream was originally made from mangoes taken from trees in the Menger's courtyard. It has been a menu staple for over a hundred years.

MAKES 1½ QUARTS

3 cups pureed mangos (from a can without the syrup)

1 tablespoon lemon juice

½ cup sugar

1 egg yolk

3 cups heavy cream

Pour the ingredients into the bowl of an ice cream machine and spin for 30 minutes to freeze.

SOPAPILLAS

1935, LA PLACITA DINING ROOMS, ALBUQUERQUE, NEW MEXICO

La Placita has ties to one of the oldest buildings in Albuquerque and was one of the first structures to be built there. In 1706 the Church of San Felipe de Neri was erected on the north side of the Plaza. Not long after the church was built, the wealthy Armijo family built their family home on the east side of the Plaza. The old adobe hacienda contained hand-carved wooden doorways and deep-sunk windows, and the old patio housed La Placita. The restaurant opened in 1935 and offered American meals like steak, chicken, and fish, but their specialty was authentic Mexican cuisine, including enchiladas, chiles rellenos, tamales, frijoles, chili con carne, and tostadas.

In 1954 Harold and Dale Elliott leased the business from Mrs. Sewell, who was in the process of remodeling the entire building. Mrs. Sewell owned and even copyrighted the name "La Placita," and transferred it to this new establishment. The Elliott brothers also owned the Court Café, Bakery and Cocktail Lounge in downtown Albuquerque. Harold told a reporter that the restaurant would have all the traditions of the old Spanish atmosphere and both Mexican and American food would be served. He noted, "Waitresses will be dressed in colorful Spanish costumes . . . and there will be music during the evening hours." They hired Albuquerque native Frank Martinez as their chef, who had recently gained national publicity while working at El Poche in San Gabriel, California. La Placita served these sopapillas, which are a Mexican type of doughnut that's traditionally filled with honey. They were so popular that they sold a sopapilla mix in their restaurant.

MAKES 16 SOPAPILLAS

2 cups flour

1 teaspoon baking powder

½ teaspoon salt

3 tablespoons lard or butter

¾ cup water

Oil, for frying

1. Mix the flour, baking powder, and salt together in a medium bowl.

2. Cut in the lard until crumbly, then add the water and mix until smooth.

3. Roll the dough into a square or rectangle on a lightly floured surface until thin like a piecrust. Cut into 3-inch squares.

4. Heat 4 inches of oil in a sturdy pot over medium-high heat until temperature reaches 375°F.

5. Gently add the dough pieces, one at a time, and fry until puffy and golden brown, about 15 seconds per side. Drain on paper towels.

CARAMELS

1870, THE BROOKVILLE HOTEL, BROOKVILLE, KANSAS

In 1870 the Kansas Pacific Railroad arrived in Brookville. Once that happened, businesses, like the Brookville Hotel, began to prosper. In 1894 Swedish native Gustav "Gus" Magnuson purchased the hotel and welcomed guests for more than thirty years. Gus and his wife Mae's daughter, Helen Martin, started working there in 1914 when she was eighteen, and began offering a family-style dining menu. She took the business over in 1933 and worked sixty hours a week as a manager and cook.

The restaurant was so popular that it was included in the 1974 edition of the Ford Motor Company's cookbook of famous recipes. The book noted, "The sign over the door to the

kitchen reads, 'Only Good Food and Pleasant People Pass Through This Door,'" and that they served an excellent family-style dinner, complete "with old-fashioned trimmings." This candy was one of their popular treats.

MAKES 64 1-INCH SQUARES

1 (15-ounce) can sweetened condensed milk

½ cup heavy cream

1 cup corn syrup

1 cup whole milk

2 cups sugar

4 tablespoons butter

2 teaspoons vanilla

1 cup pecans

1. Combine all of the ingredients except the vanilla and pecans in a large saucepan.

2. Cook over medium heat, stirring constantly, until the mixture reads 245°F on a candy thermometer or it reaches a firm ball stage when dropped in cold water.

3. Remove from the heat and add the vanilla.

4. Pour half of the mixture into a buttered 8 x 8-inch pan and sprinkle with pecans. Top with the remaining caramel mixture.

5. Allow to cool and when firm, invert the caramel onto a board and cut it with a thin knife.

6. Refrigerate for 2 hours and then wrap pieces in waxed paper.

PRALINE TULIPE

1889, BLENNERHASSETT HOTEL,
PARKERSBURG, WEST VIRGINIA

In 1883 Colonel William Nelson Chancellor began construction of the Blennerhassett Hotel, and it took six years to build. The grand opening was held on Monday, May 6, 1889, in the bustling city of Parkersburg, West Virginia. Chancellor achieved his goal of having a grand hotel for the rich because the city was in the middle of an oil and gas boom. Parkersburg's street lights were electrified in 1888, and the hotel generated its illumination with natural gas. The hotel had both gas and electric at the time that it opened. Local Parkersburg companies wired the hotel for electricity, plumbed it, and fitted it throughout with gas lighting and steam heating. The hotel had an electric passenger elevator, as well as an electric service elevator, at the time of its opening, something new for the day.

The first proprietor to lease the new hotel from Chancellor was George C. Campbell. He originally named his business the Hotel Argyle, but he eventually decided on the Hotel Blennerhassett, in honor of Harmon Blennerhassett, an Irish aristocrat who, with his family, settled on an island in the Ohio River a few miles from Parkersburg in the late eighteenth

century. The Bentley and Gerwig furniture company helped to furnish the hotel with some of its new furnishings. Chancellor had two different companies from Cincinnati, Ohio, come in and do all of the original window treatments throughout the hotel, as well as all of the frescoing works, which would have been seen in different parts of the lobby area as well as in the restaurant.

The restaurant was located on the second floor and could seat up to eighty guests at one time. The kitchen was located on the fifth floor of the new hotel in case a fire broke out—its logic being that it would start at the top of the building and work its way down—which was a common safety precaution at the time. It's believed that this signature dessert has been served at the hotel since its opening.

SERVES 10

½ cup plus 2 tablespoons butter

1 cup brown sugar

½ cup plus 2 tablespoons corn syrup

2¼ cups pecans

1 cup granulated sugar

1½ cups all-purpose flour

10 scoops praline ice cream

1¼ cups chocolate sauce

Whipped cream

20 whole strawberries

10 round chocolate wafers

10 mint sprigs

1. Melt the butter in a saucepan over low heat. Add the brown sugar and then the corn syrup, the pecans, the white sugar, and finally the flour, stirring after each addition. Cook over medium heat for 12 minutes, stirring to avoid scorching.

2. Cover two sheet pans with buttered wax or parchment paper. Place five scoops of the mixture on each of the sheets, with the dollops spaced equally to allow for spreading.

3. Bake at 325°F for 15 minutes or until golden brown. Remove from the oven and cool for 1 minute.

4. Remove each portion and place them on an upside-down soup cup (like a coffee cup with no handles). Let the praline shell sit for 3 minutes.

5. Place shell in the center of a dinner plate and place one scoop of ice cream into the shell. Ladle chocolate sauce over the ice cream, and garnish with whipped cream, two strawberries, a chocolate wafer, and a sprig of mint.

SWEDISH CREAM

1885, LUTSEN RESORT, LUTSEN, MINNESOTA

This dessert recipe dates back to the original Nelson family and has been passed down through and from the resort. For a detailed history of Lutsen Resort, see the Swedish Meatballs recipe.

MAKES 5 (4-OUNCE) PORTIONS

1 cup heavy cream

½ cup sugar

1½ gelatin sheets

1 cup sour cream

¼ teaspoon almond extract

¾ teaspoon vanilla extract

2 ounces butter

1 ounce flour

6 ounces gingersnaps, broken into chunks

1 ounce almonds, toasted

Lingonberry preserves

Whipped cream

Fresh berries

1. Heat the cream in a saucepan over low heat. Add the sugar and stir to dissolve.

2. Bloom the gelatin sheets in iced water and let sit for 3 to 4 minutes. Remove and squeeze out excess water.

3. Add the gelatin to the heated cream and sugar and stir to dissolve.

4. Place the sour cream and almond and vanilla extracts in a bowl and mix well. Add the cream mixture and blend well.

5. Divide into 4 ounces and place in glass serving cups. Allow to set in the refrigerator for 1 hour.

6. To make the streusel topping, combine the butter, flour, gingersnaps, and almonds and place onto a baking sheet. Bake at 350°F for 5 to 8 minutes.

7. To assemble the dessert, top the chilled custard with a layer of lingonberry preserves, then a layer of streusel, and finish with whipped cream and fresh berries

SWEDISH RICE PUDDING

1955, MORRIS BRYANT SMORGASBORD, LAFAYETTE, INDIANA

Smorgasbord is a Swedish word used to describe food served buffet-style at a restaurant and was added to many restaurants' names as the concept became trendy. Smorgasbords became popular in the United States in the 1930s and lasted well into the '60s and '70s until the term *buffet* replaced the Swedish term. It was the winter of 1955 when the Morris Bryant Smorgasbord opened in the Morris Bryant Hotel, which was opened in 1951. Morris Crain hired Chef Clifford Wolf to manage all of the highly trained chefs who served about seventy different items for dinner. In 1956 they began offering breakfast, lunch, and dinner smorgasbords. They also offered a champagne brunch every Sunday, and this delicious rice pudding was one of their specialties.

SERVES 10

½ **cup uncooked rice**

¼ **cup crushed pineapple**

2 **eggs**

3 **tablespoons sugar**

2 **cups milk**

½ **teaspoon vanilla**

Drop of yellow food coloring, optional

Grape jelly or preserves

1. Cook the rice according to package directions. When done, add the pineapple and set aside.

2. Place the eggs in a bowl and beat until blended. While mixing at slow speed, gradually add the sugar. Add the milk, vanilla, and food coloring while still mixing.

3. Pour the rice mixture into the egg mixture and stir to combine.

4. Pour into a greased baking dish so that the mixture is 1 inch deep. Bake at 365°F for 2 hours.

5. Serve hot or cold, topped with grape jelly or preserves.

Long-time Morris Bryant Smörgåsbord Chef Clifford Wolf poses for a photo in front of his grand smorgasbord in 1971.

RECIPE CREDITS

Allegheny Mountain Trout: 1800s, The Omni Homestead Resort, Hot Springs, Virginia
Recipe courtesy of Executive Chef Todd Owen, The Omni Homestead

Almond Macaroons: 1913, Hotel Du Pont, Wilmington, Delaware
Recipe courtesy of the Hotel Du Pont

Apple Crisp: 1886, Basin Harbor, Vergennes, Vermont
Recipe courtesy of Basin Harbor

Baked Beans: 1920, Roosevelt Lodge Restaurant, Yellowstone, Wyoming
Recipe courtesy of the Roosevelt Lodge in Yellowstone National Park

Baked Lobster: 1946, Fisherman's Wharf Inn, Boothbay Harbor, Maine
Recipe adapted from The Ford Times Cookbook: Favorite Recipes from Popular American Restaurants, *1968*

Baking Powder Biscuits: 1939, Old Hundred, Southbury, Connecticut
Recipe adapted from Recipes from Old Hundred: 200 Years of New England Cooking, *1939*

Bananas Foster: 1946, Brennan's, New Orleans, Louisiana
Recipe courtesy of Brennan's

Blueberry Torte: 1912, Homewood Inn, Yarmouth, Maine
Recipe adapted from The Ford Times Cookbook: A Traveler's Guide to Good Eating at Home and on the Road, *1974*

Bocaroons: 1926, Boca Raton Inn, Boca Raton, Florida
Recipe courtesy of the Boca Raton Club

Boston Cream Pie: 1800s, Parker House, Boston, Massachusetts
Recipe courtesy of Omni Parker House Hotel

Breakfast Ride Potatoes: 1965, White Stallion Ranch, Tucson, Arizona
Recipe courtesy of White Stallion Ranch

Brownie: 1893, Palmer House, a Hilton Hotel, Chicago, Illinois
Recipe courtesy of the Palmer House Hotel

Buffalo Wings: 1964, Anchor Bar, Buffalo, New York
Recipe courtesy of Anchor Bar

Buttermilk Pancakes: 1885, Lutsen Resort, Lutsen, Minnesota
Recipe courtesy of Lutsen Resort

Butterscotch Cookies: 1930s, Graylyn Estate, Winston-Salem, North Carolina
Recipe courtesy of Graylyn Estate

Canine Rockfish: 1816, Inn at Perry Cabin, St. Michaels, Maryland
Recipe courtesy of Chef Gregory James, Inn at Perry Cabin

Caramels: 1870, The Brookville Hotel, Brookville, Kansas
Recipe adapted from The Ford Times Cookbook: A Traveler's Guide to Good Eating at Home and on the Road, *1974*

Cheese Beans a la Fallhall: 1950, Fallhall Glen Resort, Black River Falls, Wisconsin
Recipe adapted from The Ford Treasury of Favorite Recipes from Famous Eating Places, *1950*

Cheesesteak: 1930, Pat's King of Steaks, Philadelphia, Pennsylvania
Recipe courtesy of Pat's King of Steaks

Chicken a la Cacciatore: 1950, Louigi's Charcoal Broiler & Italian Specialty Restaurant, Las Vegas, Nevada
Recipe adapted from The Ford Times Cookbook: Favorite Recipes from Popular American Restaurants, *1968*

Chicken and Waffles: 1929, Miller's, Ronks, Pennsylvania
Recipe courtesy of Miller's Smorgasbord

Chicken-Fried Steak: 1910, Cattlemen's Steakhouse, Oklahoma City, Oklahoma
Recipe courtesy of Cattlemen's Steakhouse

Chicken Kama'aina: 1944, The Willows, Honolulu, Hawaii
Recipe courtesy of Honolulu Saturday Star-Bulletin, *March 26, 1955*

Chicken Pie: 1930s, Old Hundred, Southbury, Connecticut
Recipe adapted from Recipes from Old Hundred: 200 Years of New England Cooking, *1939*

Chiles Rellenos: 1926, La Fonda Hotel, Santa Fe, New Mexico
Recipe courtesy of Chef Lane Warner, La Fonda on the Plaza

Chinese-Hawaiian Barbecued Ribs: 1950, Don the Beachcomber, Waikiki Beach, Hawaii
Recipe adapted from The Ford Treasury of Favorite Recipes from Famous Eating Places, *1950*

Chocolate Chess Pie: 1960, Angus Barn, Raleigh, North Carolina
Recipe courtesy of Angus Barn

Chocolate Pecan Pie: 1929, Miller's, Ronks, Pennsylvania
Recipe courtesy of Miller's Smorgasbord

Club House Turkey Sandwich: 1891, Huber's, Portland, Oregon
Recipe courtesy of Huber's Cafe

Cobb Salad: 1926, The Brown Derby, Los Angeles, California
Recipe as remembered and prepared by Bob Walsh

Coconut Cream Pie: 1944, The Willows, Honolulu, Hawaii
Recipe courtesy of Honolulu Saturday Star-Bulletin, *March 26, 1955*

Cole Slaw: 1947, Skylight Inn, Ayden, North Carolina
Recipe reprinted with permission from Whole Hog BBQ, by Sam Jones and Daniel Vaughn, 2019

Columbia River Salmon a la Gorge: 1921, Columbia Gorge Hotel, Hood River, Oregon
Recipe adapted from The Ford Treasury of Favorite Recipes from Famous Eating Places, *1950*

Cornhusker Salad: 1926, The Cornhusker Hotel, Lincoln, Nebraska
Recipe adapted from The Ford Treasury of Favorite Recipes from Famous Eating Places, 1950

Cornish Pasty: 1906, Gamers Confectionery and Café, Butte, Montana
Recipe adapted from The Ford Times Cookbook: Favorite Recipes from Popular American Restaurants, 1968

Cornmeal Pancakes: 1852, Holbrooke Hotel, Grass Valley, California
Recipe courtesy of Chef Zachary Arenholtz, Golden Gate Saloon & Restaurant in the Holbrooke Hotel

Crab Imperial Scotch Egg: 1816, Inn at Perry Cabin, St. Michaels, Maryland
Recipe courtesy of Chef Gregory James, Inn at Perry Cabin

Crab Louie: 1942, Aggie's, Port Angeles, Washington
Recipe adapted from The Ford Times Cookbook: Favorite Recipes from Popular American Restaurants, 1968

Date Nut Bread: 1940s, The Inn at Death Valley, Death Valley, California
Recipe courtesy of the Oasis at Death Valley

Delmonico Potatoes: 1837, Delmonico's, New York, New York
Recipe adapted from The International Cook Book, by Alexander Filippini, 1914

Deviled Crab: 1881, Winkler's, Wilmington, Delaware
Recipe adapted from The Ford Treasury of Favorite Recipes from Famous Eating Places, 1950

Diamondback Cocktail: 1928, Lord Baltimore Hotel, Baltimore, Maryland
Recipe courtesy of the Lord Baltimore Hotel

Dollar Pancakes: 1950, Picket Post Guest Ranch, Superior, Arizona
Recipe adapted from The Ford Treasury of Favorite Recipes from Famous Eating Places, 1950

Don's Big Mess: 1936, White's Restaurant, Salem, Oregon
Recipe created by Sherry Monahan based on ingredient list supplied by White's Restaurant

Eggs Benedict: 1837, Delmonico's, New York, New York
Recipe adapted from The Epicurean, by Charles Ranhofer, 1894

Escalloped Corn: 1904, Club Continental in the Jefferson Hotel, St. Louis, Missouri
Recipe adapted from the St. Louis Post-Dispatch, October 11, 1933

French-Fried Onions: 1946, Johnnie & Kay's, Des Moines, Iowa
Recipe adapted from The Ford Treasury of Favorite Recipes from Famous Eating Places, 1952

Fried Chicken: 1803, Golden Lamb, Lebanon, Ohio
Recipe courtesy of the Golden Lamb

Fried Chicken Castañeda: 1898, La Castañeda, Las Vegas, New Mexico
Recipe adapted from Santa Fe Employees' Magazine, vol. 4, June–November 1910

German Potato Salad: 1890s, Alpine Inn, Hill City, South Dakota
Recipe courtesy of Alpine Inn

Gold Brick Sundae: 1928, Sea Island Resort, Sea Island, Georgia
Recipe courtesy of Sea Island Resort

Green Chile Philly: 1971, Chute Rooster, Hill City, South Dakota
Recipe courtesy of Chute Rooster

Green Enchiladas: 1946, Casa Rio, San Antonio, Texas
Recipe courtesy of Casa Rio

Green Goddess Dressing: 1875, Palace Hotel, San Francisco, California
Recipe courtesy of the Palace Hotel

Honey Carrots: 1937, Sun Valley Resort, Sun Valley, Idaho
Recipe courtesy of the Ram Restaurant at Sun Valley Resort

Hot Brown: 1923, The Brown Hotel, Louisville, Kentucky
Recipe courtesy of the Brown Hotel

Huckleberry Muffins: 1886, Crescent Hotel & Spa, Eureka Springs, Arkansas
Recipe adapted from The Ford Treasury of Favorite Recipes from Famous Eating Places, *1950*

Hungarian Goulash: 1937, Sun Valley Resort, Sun Valley, Idaho
Recipe courtesy of the Ram Restaurant in Sun Valley Resort

Husky King Crab Boat: 1960, Fairbanks Inn, Fairbanks, Alaska
Recipe adapted from The Ford Times Cookbook: A Traveler's Guide to Good Eating at Home and on the Road, *1974*

Jonny Cakes: 1755, Kingston Inn, Kingston, Rhode Island
Recipe adapted from Duncan Hines' Adventures in Good Cooking and the Art of Carving in the Home, *1952*

The Jucy Lucy: 1954, Matt's Bar, Minneapolis, Minnesota
Recipe courtesy of Matt's Bar & Grill

Lamb Bolognese: 1882, Twin Lakes Inn, Twin Lakes, Colorado
Recipe courtesy of Twin Lakes Inn

Lamb Fries: 1910, Cattlemen's Steakhouse, Oklahoma City, Oklahoma
Recipe courtesy of Cattlemen's Steakhouse

Lamb Shanks: 1919, The Martin Hotel, Winnemucca, Nevada
Recipe courtesy of John Arant of the Martin Hotel

Lobster a la Newberg: 1830, Delmonico's, New York, New York
Recipe adapted from The Epicurean, *by Charles Ranhofer, 1894*

Mai Tai: 1944, Trader Vic's, Oakland, California
Recipe from Trader Vic's Bartender's Guide, *Revised, 1972*

Mango Ice Cream: 1859, Menger Hotel, San Antonio, Texas
Recipe courtesy of the Menger Hotel

Manhattan Clam Chowder: 1938, Dunleavy's Restaurant and Cocktail Lounge, Hainesport, New Jersey
Recipe from the author

Maple Muffins: 1920, Maple Cabin, St. Johnsbury, Vermont
Recipe adapted from Duncan Hines' Adventures in Good Cooking and the Art of Carving in the Home, *1939*

Marinated Pork Chops: 1958 The Embers, Mt. Pleasant, Michigan
Recipe adapted from The Ford Times Cookbook: Favorite Recipes from Popular American Restaurants, *1968*
Maryland-Style Fried Chicken: 1928, Lord Baltimore Hotel, Baltimore, Maryland
Recipe courtesy of the Lord Baltimore Hotel
Melon Soup: 1948, Ruby Chow's Chinese Dinner Club, Seattle, Washington
Recipe adapted from The Ford Treasury of Favorite Recipes from Famous Eating Places, *1950*
Mint Julep: 1847, Willard Hotel, Washington, DC
Recipe courtesy of the Willard Hotel
Navajo Tacos: 1925, Zion Lodge, Springdale, Utah
Recipe courtesy of Zion National Park
New England Clam Chowder: 1826, Union Oyster House, Boston, Massachusetts
Recipe adapted from The Ford Treasury of Favorite Recipes from Famous Eating Places, *1950*
New Jersey Sloppy Joe: 1927, Town Hall Delicatessen, South Orange, New Jersey
Recipe courtesy of Town Hall Deli
Oysters Rockefeller & Bienville: 1840, Antoine's, New Orleans, Louisiana
Recipe courtesy of Antoine's
Parker House Rolls: 1856, Parker House, Boston, Massachusetts
Recipe courtesy of Omni Parker House
Peanut Soup: 1882, Hotel Roanoke, Roanoke, Virginia
Recipe courtesy of the Hotel Roanoke

Pecan Ball: 1887, Grand Hotel, Mackinac Island, Michigan
Recipe courtesy of the Grand Hotel
Pecan Pie: 1910, Partridge Inn, Augusta, Georgia
Recipe courtesy of Chef Thomas Jacobs, Partridge Inn
Pheasant: 1940s, Chef Louie's Steak House, Mitchell, South Dakota
Recipe adapted from The Ford Times Cookbook: Favorite Recipes from Popular American Restaurants, *1968*
Pickled Shrimp: 1947, Villula Tea Garden, Seale, Alabama
Recipe adapted from The Ford Times Cookbook: Favorite Recipes from Popular American Restaurants, *1968*
Po'boy (Poor Boy) Sandwich: 1929, Parkway Bakery & Tavern, New Orleans, Louisiana
Recipe courtesy of Parkway Bakery & Tavern
Praline Tulipe: 1889, Blennerhassett Hotel, Parkersburg, West Virginia
Recipe courtesy of the Blennerhassett Hotel
Prickly Pear Margarita: 1990, White Stallion Ranch, Tucson, Arizona
Recipe courtesy of White Stallion Ranch
Prime Rib: 1952, Brown Palace Hotel, Denver, Colorado
Recipe courtesy of Brown Palace Hotel
Pumpkin Bread: 1796, Fitzwilliam Inn, Fitzwilliam, New Hampshire
Recipe courtesy of the Fitzwilliam Inn
Relish: 1922, Sawyer Tavern, Keene, New Hampshire
Recipe adapted from Duncan Hines' Adventures in Good Cooking and the Art of Carving in the Home, *1945*

Rice Mangalais with Curry Sauce: 1904, Club Continental in the Jefferson Hotel, St. Louis, Missouri
Recipe adapted from The Ford Treasury of Favorite Recipes from Famous Eating Places, *1950*

Russian Dressing: 1968, Marina Inn, Sioux City, Nebraska
Recipe adapted from The Ford Times Cookbook: A Traveler's Guide to Good Eating at Home and on the Road, *1974*

Sauerkraut Balls: 1803, Golden Lamb, Lebanon, Ohio
Recipe courtesy of the Golden Lamb

Scalloped Eggplant: 1834, J. Huston Tavern, Arrow Rock, Missouri
Recipe adapted from The Ford Treasury of Favorite Recipes from Famous Eating Places, *1950*

Sea Salt Chocolate Chip Cookies: 1816, Inn at Perry Cabin, St. Michaels, Maryland
Recipe courtesy of Chef Gregory James and the Inn at Perry Cabin

She Crab Soup: 1763, John Rutledge House Inn, Charleston, South Carolina
Recipe adapted from 200 Years of Charleston Cooking, *by Blanche Salley-Rhett, 1930*

Shenandoah Apple Pie: 1931, The Mimslyn Inn, Luray, Virginia
Recipe courtesy of the Mimslyn Inn

Sherried Mushrooms: 1937, Sun Valley Resort, Sun Valley, Idaho
Recipe courtesy of the Ram Restaurant at Sun Valley Resort

Shrimp Cocktail: 1902, St. Elmo Steak House, Indianapolis, Indiana
Recipe courtesy of St. Elmo Steak House

Shrimp Salad Louis Stratta: 1918, The Broadmoor, Colorado Springs, Colorado
Recipe courtesy of the Broadmoor Hotel

Sister Lizzie's Shaker Sugar Pie: 1803, Golden Lamb, Lebanon, Ohio
Recipe courtesy of the Golden Lamb

Sonoran Spice Brisket: 1965, White Stallion Ranch, Tucson, Arizona
Recipe courtesy of White Stallion Ranch

Sopapillas: 1935, La Placita Dining Rooms, Albuquerque, New Mexico
Recipe adapted from The Ford Treasury of Favorite Recipes from Famous Eating Places, *1950*

Sour Schmorrbraten (Sauerbraten): 1904, Club Continental in the Jefferson Hotel, St. Louis,
Recipe adapted from the St. Louis Star-Times, *May 20, 1937*

Spaetzle: 1937, Sun Valley Resort, Sun Valley, Idaho
Recipe courtesy of the Ram Restaurant at Sun Valley Resort

Spaghetti and Meatballs: 1900, Ralph's Italian Restaurant, Philadelphia, Pennsylvania
Recipe courtesy of Ralph's

Spoon Bread: 1926, The Westin Poinsett Hotel, Greenville, South Carolina
Recipe courtesy of the Westin Poinsett Hotel

Stone-Ground Meal Pancakes: 1946, The Country Store Restaurant, Weston, Vermont
Recipe adapted from The Ford Times Cookbook: A Traveler's Guide to Good Eating at Home and on the Road, *1974*

Stuffed Peppers, Creole Style: 1941, Old Southern Tea Room, Vicksburg, Mississippi
Recipe adapted from The Ford Treasury of Favorite Recipes from Famous Eating Places, *1950*

Swedish Collops (Swedish Beef Stew): 1918, Norton Hotel, Detroit, Michigan
Recipe adapted from The Ford Treasury of Favorite Recipes from Famous Eating Places, *1950*

Swedish Cream: 1885, Lutsen Resort, Lutsen, Minnesota
Recipe courtesy of Lutsen Resort

Swedish Meatballs: 1885, Lutsen Resort, Lutsen, Minnesota
Recipes courtesy of Lutsen Resort

Swedish Rice Pudding: 1955, Morris Bryant Smorgasbord, Lafayette, Indiana
Recipe adapted from Ford Times Favorite Recipes: A Traveler's Guide to Good Eating on the Road and at Home, *1979*

Thomas Jefferson's Vanilla Ice Cream: 1930, Pride Dairy, Bottineau, North Dakota
Recipe adapted from Thomas Jefferson, Ice Cream Recipe, no date (Manuscript/Mixed Material), retrieved from the Library of Congress

Trout Amandine: 1882, Twin Lakes Inn, Twin Lakes, Colorado
Recipe courtesy of Twin Lakes Inn

Vanilla Bourbon Ice Cream: 1931, The Mimslyn Inn, Luray, Virginia
Recipe courtesy of Chef Chris Harris, Mimslyn Inn

Vanilla Muffins: 1869, The Peabody, Memphis, Tennessee
Recipe adapted from the Boston Herald, *February 29, 1928*

Vichyssoise: 1910, Ritz-Carlton Hotel, New York, New York
Recipe from Louis Diat, which appeared in Look *magazine, June 16, 1953*

Waffles: 1929, Miller's, Ronks, Pennsylvania
Recipe courtesy of Miller's Smorgasbord

Waldorf Salad: 1893, Waldorf-Astoria, New York, New York
Recipe adapted from The Cook Book by Oscar of The Waldorf, *by Oscar Tschirky, 1896*

White Chocolate Chip Cookies: 1965, White Stallion Ranch, Tucson, Arizona
Recipe courtesy of White Stallion Ranch

Zombie: 1934, Don the Beachcomber, Hollywood, California
Recipe from Trader Vic's Book of Food & Drink, *1946*

IMAGE CREDITS

Page 5

Photo courtesy of White's

Pages 10, 11

Photos courtesy of Chef Zachary Arenholtz, Golden Gate Saloon & Restaurant in the Holbrooke Hotel

Page 12

Photo courtesy of Lutsen Inn

Page 13

Photo courtesy of Miller's Smorgasbord

Pages 15, 16

Photos courtesy of Omni Parker House

Page 21

Photo courtesy of the Oasis at Death Valley

Page 23

Photo courtesy of the author

Page 25

Photo from Wikipedia

Page 27

Image from the Caledonia-Record, *1950*

Page 30

Photo courtesy of White Stallion Ranch

Page 33

Photo courtesy of Antoine's

Page 35

Photo courtesy of St. Elmo Steak House

Page 36

Image from The Ford Times Cookbook: Favorite Recipes from Popular American Restaurants, *1968*

Pages 39, 41

Photo courtesy of Chef Gregory James, Inn at Perry Cabin

Page 42

Image from The Ford Times Cookbook: A Traveler's Guide to Good Eating at Home and on the Road, *1974*

Page 43

Image from the Culinary Institute of America Menu Collection; Bruce P. Jeffer Menu Collection

Page 45

Photo courtesy of Anchor Bar

Page 46

Image from the Honolulu Star-Bulletin, *May 17, 1946*

Page 49

Photo courtesy of the Golden Lamb

Page 52

Photo courtesy of Cattlemen's Steakhouse

Page 53

Image from The Ford Treasury of Favorite Recipes from Famous Eating Places, *1950*

Page 55

Photo courtesy of the author

Page 57

Image from the Miriam and Ira D. Wallach Division of Art, Prints and Photographs: Print Collection, The New York Public Library

Page 59

Photo from the Roanoke Times, *August 20, 1951*

Page 62

Photo from Look *magazine, December 1953*

Page 65

Photo from the Miriam and Ira D. Wallach Division of Art, Prints and Photographs: Picture Collection, The New York Public Library.

Page 67

Photo from the Lincoln Star, July 4, 1926

Page 70

Photo courtesy of the Broadmoor Hotel

Page 72

Image from The Ford Times Cookbook: Favorite Recipes from Popular American Restaurants, *1968*

Page 75

Photo from Wikipedia

Page 79

Photo from the Lincoln Evening Journal, *November 29, 1968*

Page 80

Photo courtesy of the Palace Hotel

Page 84

Image from The Epicurean, *by Charles Ranhofer, 1894*

Page 86

Photo from the Des Moines Tribune, *November 23, 1976*

Page 90

Image from The Ford Treasury of Favorite Recipes from Famous Eating Places, *1950*

Page 92

Image from The LaCrosse Sunday Tribune, *August 30, 1959*

Page 94

Photo courtesy of the Roosevelt Lodge in Yellowstone National Park

Page 97

Photo by Denny Culbert; published by Ten Speed Press, a division of Penguin Random House, Inc.

Page 100

Photo from Look *magazine, December, 1953*

Page 101

Photo from the St. Louis Post-Dispatch, *July 17, 1955*

Page 104

Photo courtesy of Town Hall Deli

Page 106

Photo courtesy of Pat's King of Steaks

Page 107

Photo courtesy of Chute Rooster

Page 108

Photo courtesy of American Coney Island

Page 109

Photo courtesy of Huber's Cafe

Page 111

Photo courtesy of Matt's Bar & Grill

Page 113

Photo courtesy of the Brown Hotel

Page 114

Photo courtesy of the Willard Hotel

Page 116

Photo courtesy of Parkway Bakery & Tavern

Page 118

Image from the Daily Argus-Leader, *March 6, 1955*

Page 120

Photo from the Library of Congress, Farm Security Administration, Office of War Information Black-and-White Negatives

Page 121

Photo courtesy of the Lord Baltimore Hotel

Page 122

Photo courtesy of the Golden Lamb

Page 125

Image from the Culinary Institute of America Menu Collection, Bruce P. Jeffer Menu Collection

Page 127

Image from Rare Book Division, The New York Public Library, Digital Collections, 1960

Page 130

Photo courtesy of UNLV

Page 132

Image from the Miriam and Ira D. Wallach Division of Art, Prints and Photographs: Print Collection, The New York Public Library

Page 134

Photo courtesy of Miller's Smorgasbord

Page 136

Photo courtesy of Casa Rio

Page 140

Image from The Ford Times Cookbook: Favorite Recipes from Popular American Restaurants, *1968*

Page 142

Image from The Ford Treasury of Favorite Recipes from Famous Eating Places, *1950*

Page 144

Photo courtesy of Executive Chef Todd Owen, The Omni Homestead

Page 147

Photo courtesy of Twin Lakes Inn

Page 149

Image from The Ford Treasury of Favorite Recipes from Famous Eating Places, *1950*

Page 150

Photo courtesy of Cattlemen's Steakhouse

Page 152

Photo from the Montana Standard, *November 7, 1950*

Page 154

Photo from the St. Louis Post Dispatch, *August 16, 1929*

Page 156

Photo courtesy of Ralph's

Page 158

Image from the Detroit Free Press, *August 12, 1945*

Page 162

Photo courtesy of Lutsen Resort

Page 163

Photo courtesy of Brown Palace Hotel

Page 165

Photo courtesy of White Stallion Ranch

Page 166

Photo courtesy of White Stallion Ranch

Page 167

Photo courtesy of the Ram Restaurant in Sun Valley Resort

Page 171

Photo courtesy of Twin Lakes Inn

Page 173

Image from the State Journal, *February 21, 1970*

Page 176

Photo courtesy of Zion National Park

Page 180

Photo courtesy of Omni Parker House Hotel

Page 182

Photo courtesy of Golden Lamb

Page 184

Photo courtesy of Angus Barn

Page 186

Photo courtesy of the author

Page 189

Photo courtesy of Miller's Smorgasbord

Page 190

Photo courtesy of the Mimslyn Inn

Page 192

Image from the Honolulu Advertiser, *February 23, 1961*

Page 194

Photo courtesy of Basin Harbor

Page 197

Image from the Evening Express, *July 10, 1963*

Page 198

Photo courtesy of the Palmer House Hotel

Page 201

Photo courtesy of Brennan's

Page 203

Photo courtesy of the Boca Raton Club

Page 205

Photo courtesy of White Stallion Ranch

Page 206

Photo courtesy of the author

Page 208

Photo courtesy of the Hotel Du Pont

Page 210

Photo courtesy of the Grand Hotel

Page 212

Photo courtesy of Sea Island Resort

Page 215

Photo from Thomas Jefferson, early 1800s (Manuscript/Mixed Material), retrieved from the Library of Congress

Page 216

Photo courtesy of the Mimslyn Inn

Page 218

Photo courtesy of the Menger Hotel

Page 221

Image from The Ford Treasury of Favorite Recipes from Famous Eating Places, *1950*

Page 222

Image from The Ford Times Cookbook: A Traveler's Guide to Good Eating at Home and on the Road, *1974*

Page 224

Photo courtesy of the Blennerhassett Hotel

Page 226

Photo courtesy of Lutsen Resort

Page 242

Photo courtesy of Sheryl Kirksey

INDEX

ABOUT THE AUTHOR

Sherry Monahan is a culinary historian who enjoys researching the genealogy of food and spirits. After studying frontier food, her culinary repertoire has expanded to include food and drinks from all over America and beyond. She holds memberships in the James Beard Foundation, the Authors Guild, the Single Action Shooting Society, and the Wild West History Association. She is the past president of Western Writers of America (2014–2016), a professional genealogist, an honorary Dodge City marshal, and a member of the Most Intrepid Western Author Posse. Her other publications include *The Tombstone Cookbook*; *Mrs. Earp: The Wives & Lovers of the Earp Brothers*; *Frontier Fare*; *Tinsel, Tumbleweeds, and Star-Spangled Celebrations*; and *The Golden Elixir of the West*. She lives in North Carolina.